NUTRITION
IN A CHANGING WORLD

James Rye
Lily Hsu O'Connell
Paul E. Bell

A Curriculum for Grade 5

NUTRITION
IN A CHANGING WORLD

This curriculum has been a collaborative effort of
the College of Education and the College of
Human Development at The Pennsylvania State
University, sponsored by the Nutrition
Foundation and supported by the Heinz
Endowment.

The School Nutrition Education Curriculum Study
was under the direction of Helen Guthrie
and Barbara Shannon.

NUTRITION
IN A CHANGING WORLD

A Curriculum for Grade 5.

James Rye
Lily Hsu O'Connell
Paul E. Bell

Brigham Young University Press

Worksheets in this book may be duplicated for nonprofit use.

Library of Congress Cataloging in Publication Data

Rye, James.
  Nutrition in a changing world, for grade five.

  "The School Nutrition Education Curriculum Study."
  "A collaborative effort of the College of Education
and the College of Human Development at the Pennsylvania
State University."
  Bibliography: p.
  1. Nutrition—Study and teaching (Elementary)
I. O'Connell, Lily Hsu, joint author. II. Bell, Paul E., joint
author. III. Pennsylvania. State University.
College of Education. IV. Pennsylvania. State
University. College of Human Development. V. Title.
VI. Title: School Nutrition Education Curriculum Study.
TX364.025   372.3'7   80-28167
ISBN 0-8425-1916-5   AACR1

Library of Congress Catalog Card Number: 80-28167
International Standard Book Number: 0-8425-1916-5
Brigham Young University Press, Provo, Utah 84602
© 1981 Brigham Young University Press. All rights reserved
Printed in the United States of America
3/81 49932

Contents

Acknowledgments

This curriculum has been a collaborative effort of the College of Education and the College of Human Development at The Pennsylvania State University.

We acknowledge those who contributed to the production of the curriculum materials comprising *Nutrition in a Changing World* for use with fifth-grade students.

We especially thank Karen Carlson, Elaine S. Ficker, Susan L. Kennedy, Martha Plass, Cindy Sherwood, Malle Sibul, Leslie Turner, and Edward Weiss for their literary contributions; Anne Van Zelst and Carolyn Haa for graphic arts concepts; Barbara Hunt for her resource review; Richard Rodibaugh, William Bernazolli and Richard Schultz, fifth-grade teachers, for lesson review; and Norma Woika and Nancy Erdley for preparation of the manuscript.

Introduction to the Fifth-Grade Curriculum

Children in the intermediate grades are in dynamic stages of growth. Some of the girls will begin to take on the characteristics of puberty during these years. The boys, lagging behind generally, will have erratic spurts of growth. All students are very conscious about who is bigger, stronger, and faster. Simultaneously, they are keeping a covetous eye on those siblings and neighbors who have already entered the teen years. Virtually everyone wants to be "big," which means "not being a little kid." Therefore, growth is a prime preoccupation of intermediate age students.

Growth is an encompassing study. It is an integral part of nutrition, and this curriculum continues the pattern of linking physiology with nutrients and foods. The learning activities encourage high student involvement in a variety of ways. Each lesson provides practice for application of earlier acquired skills to new situations or problems.

The curriculum for grade five develops the following concepts:

- Two determinants of growth—which involves many different processes—are diet and heredity.
- Energy needs are dependent on growth, body size and composition, sex, age, environment, and physical activity.
- Energy equilibrium promotes optimum growth and health.
- Energy is derived from carbohydrates, protein, fat; the latter is the most concentrated source.
- Sugars are a type of carbohydrate found in many foods.
- Frequent consumption of high sugar foods increases the chance of the formation of plaque on the teeth, with subsequent tooth decay.
- Orally safe snack foods include fresh fruits and vegetables, unsweetened juices, milk, cheese, and nuts.
- Protein, which can be used for energy, primarily functions as the supplier of building materials for tissue growth, repair, and maintenance.
- Cultural and environmental factors strongly influence the kinds of food in a population's diet.

How to Use Nutrition in a Changing World, Grade Five

This curriculum has been designed to follow in sequence the primary and grade four levels of Nutrition in a Changing World. It has been divided into twenty-one lessons that should be taught in sequence. The

1

first lesson serves as a review of the functions and food sources of iron, calcium, protein, vitamin A, and vitamin C. These nutrients are collectively called Iron CaPAC and were first introduced in the grade four level of the curriculum. Each lesson has been designed to include flexibility to fit various situations and the capabilities of the students. Teachers who critiqued pilot lessons identified two specifications for the intermediate grade level: that although the knowledge of the way the human body works is important in understanding nutrition, each lesson must obviously include some attention to one or more nutrients; and that crowded curricula demand nutrition lessons be used in conjunction with established areas of study, such as science, mathematics, and language arts.

Each lesson attempts to relate knowledge of the human body and nutrient interaction in meaningful terms. Each lesson also identifies an *interdisciplinary emphasis,* that is, a subject area with which the nutrition lesson could best be interrelated. The orchestration of the nutrition lesson with the interdisciplinary emphasis will help ease the crowded curriculum.

Following the interdisciplinary emphasis, each lesson identifies the nutrition *concept* that is developed; usually only one is presented. This clearly and concisely delineates to the teacher what is to be taught. After the concept, an *objective* is identified. The objective states how the student should perform to give evidence that he or she has learned the concept.

Within each lesson, information pertinent to that area of nutrition is included as *nutrition information.* This provides supplementary and background information for the teacher so that the purpose of the lesson and the activity are understood. Words or short phrases found in italics in this section of the lesson refer to terms listed in the *glossary.*

The next section of each lesson is entitled *activity.* Most of these activities are experientially oriented and each is designed to take approximately forty minutes of student classroom time. If an activity requires more time, the teacher is alerted. To facilitate the teacher's preparation time, many of the student written materials (worksheets and charts) have been designed, and master copies are included. Students will be able to complete many of the worksheets independently, while others will be more effective if students are guided through the worksheet. The teacher simply duplicates the quantity needed. The titles of these materials are printed under the subsection Materials Needed. Any of these materials may be found either at the end of the lesson or in the appendixes. For successful nutrition instruction, students must be actively involved in making decisions with real foods or at least realistic pictures of foods; it is therefore recommended that a set of food models be obtained.* These are lifelike and can be used for establishing portion sizes. In addition to the realism of the photographs, these food models contain important nutrition information on the reverse side.

Sometimes an activity requires the student to complete several sequential steps. Such activities have been subdivided accordingly into Part A, Part B, Part C, and so on. These subdivisions are suggested areas for stopping if class time has run out, or for checking the students' grasp of the information presented thus far.

---

*Food Models: National Dairy Council, 6300 North River Road, Rosemont, IL 60018. Full-color photographs (B012A-146) life size, $7.00/set; full color photographs B012B-58 life size, $5.00/set.

A few of the lessons in this curriculum have an *alternate activity* that enables the students to develop the nutrition concept. The *activity* need not be conducted prior to completing the alternate activity. This freedom allows teachers to tailor nutrition lessons closer to the capabilities of the students and provides more opportunities for the class to grasp the nutrition concept. In a few instances an Additional Activity is provided, supplying supplementary material and requiring that the activity be conducted beforehand.

Each lesson has a section devoted to *evaluation*. Short-answer quiz items pertain to the concept presented in the lesson. Many of the activities also have been designed to be used as a means of student evaluation. In any case, these modes of evaluation are simply suggestions and do not necessarily need to be followed.

At the end of the curriculum a section has been devoted to *references/resources*. For each lesson, materials of various media for students and teachers are listed, along with the addresses where these materials can be obtained. The materials for students are designated by (S) and for teachers by (T). These suggested materials are nutritionally accurate and appropriate. Teachers should be critical of new nutritional materials as they appear on the market.

Appendix J is a Nutrition Knowledge test concerning the concepts taught in these lessons and may be used as a pre/post assessment of a student's understanding of the material. An answer key is provided.

The complexity of nutrition prevents us from providing simple answers. We hope this curriculum will help teachers and students learn about the relationship between nutrition and health. The lessons presented here are cumulative. Consequently, as students proceed through the curriculum, their conceptual accuracy will improve with each lesson.

Development of the Curriculum

Nutrition in a Changing World is a comprehensive nutrition-education plan for preschool through grade twelve. The scope and sequence of the curriculum were developed to include teaching very young children, who need the knowledge and skills to make personal dietary decisions. The material in the curriculum has been organized into a spiral format. Preschoolers (ages three through five years) accumulate first-hand experience to broaden their perspective of what may be considered food. Attention is given to developing sensory skills in children, to familiarizing them with food variety, and to fostering in them pleasant associations with food. Primary students (grades one through three) have shown that they can indeed understand and apply nutrition concepts. Food choices are based on their nutrient content. Students examine the relationship of nutrition in various social settings. Intermediate students (grades four through six) learn how our bodies use nutrients to perform, and they learn the food sources of several nutrients. Throughout the elementary years the focus of attention is on the individual and on his or her food choices.

At the junior and senior high level the emphasis shifts to include the responsibility of dependents and the concern for national and international decisions that affect the nutrition of the students' families. These students will relate their knowledge to the concerns and different needs of other groups and of members of their family. Thus, *Nutrition in a Changing World,* as it should, taxes the cognitive capabilities of the respective learners.

3

The concepts in the curricula were identified by nutrition educators across the nation as important to learning. The curricula also include the acceptability of the Basic Four Food Groups, but recognize that adequate nutrition today requires an understanding of *nutrients* as well as food groups.

The concepts for grade five are collectively found in the Lesson Outline, which lists the content to be covered in each lesson. This outline has been provided so that the range of issues addressed in these lessons can be used as an aid in using this curriculum more effectively.

Lesson Title Outline

Interdisciplinary Emphasis	Concept	Title
Health	Iron, calcium, protein, vitamin A, and vitamin C are five nutrients that perform important functions in the human body. We refer to these five nutrients collectively as the Iron CaPAC nutrients. Some foods are better sources of the Iron CaPAC nutrients than other foods. Learning which foods are good sources of these nutrients will help young people get adequate amounts of them daily.	1. Who's on First?
Language Arts	For a body to grow in length, bones need to grow and become hard. Many nutrients are needed for bone growth. Protein, vitamin C, and iron all make collagen; phosphorus, calcium, and vitamin A help to make bones hard.	2. Knee Bone Connected to the. . . .
Language Arts Mathematics	No two healthy people grow at the same rate—this is okay.	3. Who's Bigger?
Language Arts	How tall your parents or grandparents are has a lot to do with how tall you grow. Proper nutrition and keeping well help insure that you will grow the way you should.	4. How Tall Is Your Family Tree?
Science	Our energy comes from the sun through plants and animals.	5. Energy Traps, Part I
Science Mathematics	Energy-storing chemicals in our food are the three nutrients carbohydrates, fats, and proteins.	6. Energy Traps, Part II

Title	Interdisciplinary Emphasis	Concept
7. How Does Your Body Get Energy?	Science	Enzymes are special chemicals in our body to help us get energy out of fats, carbohydrates, and proteins.
8. Putting Food Energy to Work: Part I	Health	The body uses food energy for many basic processes, such as breathing and keeping body cells alive. These basic processes are called basal metabolism. We also use energy to digest and absorb food. However, digestion and absorption are not part of basal metabolism.
9. Putting Food Energy to Work: Part II	Mathematics Health	In addition to basal metabolism, digestion, and absorption, our bodies use energy to move muscles. Muscle movement is referred to as physical activity. Over a twenty-four-hour period, the body usually uses more energy for basal metabolism than for physical activity.
10. All about Calories	Health	Calories are the units we use to measure the amount of energy in food.
11. Calorie Input versus Output	Mathematics Health	The number of Calories you take into your body should be equal to but should not exceed the number your body needs for basal metabolism, digestion, absorption of food, and physical activity.
12. Fats in Foods	Health	Fats provide more than twice as much energy as do proteins or carbohydrates. Foods high in fat are high in Calories.
13. Find the Fat	Mathematics	Animal foods tend to contain more fat than plant foods. We cannot always see the fat in a food. Hot dogs, cheese, and nuts are good examples of foods containing "hidden fat."
14. Simple versus Complex	Language Arts	The carbohydrates are a class of nutrients containing "sugars" (simple carbohydrate) and "fiber and starch" (complex carbohydrate).
15. Boxes and Cubes	Mathematics	The amount of table sugar (sucrose) in equal amounts of two different foods may vary significantly.
16. Snack Plaque Fighters I	Health	Like fat, sucrose hides in many foods. Except for fresh fruits and natural juices, snacks with hidden sucrose are not good for the teeth.

Interdisciplinary Emphasis	Concept	Title
Mathematics	Sticky, sweet foods are the most orally hazardous. Snacking on sucrose-containing foods throughout the day is more orally hazardous than eating these foods at mealtime. Examples of snacks that are orally safe include fresh fruits and vegetables, unsweetened juices, milk, cheese, and nuts.	17. Snack Plaque Fighters II
Science	Bacteria are microscopic and, like man, use the nutrients in food.	18. Bacteria
Health	Bacteria, living in plaque on our teeth, turn sugar (especially sucrose) into acid. This acid is harmful to the teeth, causing cavities.	19. Plaque, Acid, and Teeth
Mathematics	The body uses protein mainly as building blocks for growth and repair of body tissue. Protein can also be used for energy. Protein supplies as much energy as carbohydrate but less than half as much as fat.	20. Protein: First a Builder
Social Studies	People from other cultures combine foods in a variety of ways to obtain a balanced diet. Environment and cultural factors influence the preparation of the food.	21. It's a Small World

Lesson 1
Who's on First?

	Interdisciplinary Emphasis

Health

Iron, calcium, protein, vitamin A, and vitamin C are five *nutrients* that perform important functions in the human body. We refer to these five nutrients collectively as the Iron CaPAC nutrients.

Some foods are better sources of the Iron CaPAC nutrients than other foods. Learning which ones are good sources will help young people get adequate amounts of nutrients daily.

Concepts

Students will review food sources and functions of the Iron CaPAC nutrients in the body by answering the questions given in the baseball game.

Objective

In this lesson, students will review and strengthen their knowledge of the Iron CaPAC nutrients first presented in grade four. For additional background information about the Iron CaPAC nutrients you may wish to refer to the nutrition curriculum for grade four. Each of the Iron CaPAC nutrients, their food sources, and their function in the body were covered in several lessons.

This beginning lesson for grade five will lay a foundation for the concepts to be learned during the coming year.

If more review is needed, use the Alternate Activity provided.

Nutrition Information

Materials Needed
Key Nutrients in Foods (Appendix A)
Food Composition Table for Selected Foods (Appendix D)
Any food composition table (optional)

Divide the class into two teams (A and B). Draw a baseball diamond and scoreboard on the blackboard or, if you desire, on the classroom floor.

Activity

Team	Innings 1	2	3	4	5	6	7	8	9	Hits Single	Double	Triple	Homer	Outs	Runs
A															
B															

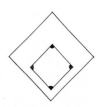

One member of the team (or you) "pitches questions to a batter" on the other team. If the batter gets the correct answer, he or she has a hit. Some questions may require two to four right answers; if so, the batter may have a double, a triple, or a home run. On the diamond, put an X beside bases held. Everyone on base moves on ahead of the batter. If the answer is incorrect, the batter is out. Each team gets three outs. You may want to set a time limit for the batter to answer, perhaps fifteen seconds.

Either you or an appointed student should be in charge of keeping the scoreboard up to date. In addition, each team member should keep track of the number of "at bats" and the number of bases he or she gets for each time at bat. You can evaluate each student's performance by dividing the number of bases by the number of times at bat.

The following questions are examples you can use, but you and the students should make up other questions.

1. What is/are (one, two, three or four) good source(s) of a) iron, b) calcium, c) protein, d) vitamin A, and e) vitamin C?
   (See Key Nutrients in Foods and Food Composition Table for Selected Nutrients, Appendixes A and D.)
2. Name one function for each of the following nutrients a) iron, b) calcium, c) protein, d) vitamin A, and e) vitamin C.
   (iron: helps blood carry oxygen)
   (calcium: builds bones and teeth; helps blood clot; helps nerves work)
   (protein: builds and repairs tissue)
   (vitamin A: necessary for growth; helps vision)
   (vitamin C: strengthens blood vessels; aids in healing; participates in bone and teeth formation)
3. What is another name for ascorbic acid? _____ (vitamin C)
4. Joe didn't like milk but he liked eating a mixed green salad with Italian dressing. Did he get any calcium? _____

   _____

   (Yes, small amounts from greens in his salad.)

Scoring:
   1 correct answer = single
   2 correct answers = double
   3 correct answers = triple
   4 correct answers = home run

Alternate Activity

Materials Needed
Matching (worksheet)

Distribute the worksheet Matching to each member of the class. This activity will test students' knowledge of food sources and bodily functions of nutrients. You may wish to add more choices or have the students create some of their own.

Answer Key to Matching:
A. Draw a line to match each pair of foods with the nutrient they provide:

peaches and carrots   calcium
Bran Flakes and raisins   iron
potatoes and oranges   protein
milk and yogurt   vitamin A
soybeans and eggs   vitamin C

B. Draw a line to match each nutrient with its function in the body.

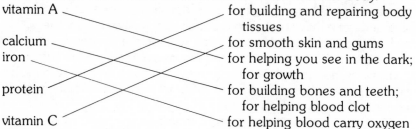

vitamin A — for building and repairing body tissues

calcium — for smooth skin and gums

iron — for helping you see in the dark; for growth

protein — for building bones and teeth; for helping blood clot

vitamin C — for helping blood carry oxygen

A mechanism for evaluating student performance is explained in the Activity. The Alternate Activity could also serve as an evaluation.

Evaluation

References and Resources

Books

O'Connell, L.; Rye, J.; and Bell, P. 1981. *Nutrition in a Changing World: A Curriculum for Grade Four.* Provo, Utah: Brigham Young University Press. (T)

Pamphlets

"Nutritive Values of Foods." 1971. Home and Garden Bulletin Number 72. Superintendent of Documents, U.S. Government Printing Office, Washington, D.C. 20402. $1.05 (T)

Posters

"Yardsticks for Nutrition." 1973. Cornell University Cooperative Extension Service, Ithaca, NY 14853. Kit of four nutrient cards/twelve card inserts, guide. 25¢ (S)

Films/Filmstrips

"Food for Thought." No date (ca. 1974–75). Marsh Film Enterprises, P.O. Box 8082, Shawnee Mission, KS 66208. Filmstrip/audiocassette, 14 minutes. $22.50 (S)

Games

"Soup's On." 1970. Didactron, P.O. Box 1501, Ann Arbor, MI 48106. $12 (S)

"Super Sandwich." 1973. Teaching Concepts, 230 Park Avenue, New York, NY 10017. (Board game.) $12.95 (S)

"Wheels." 1972. Didactron, P.O. Box 1501, Ann Arbor, MI 48106. $12 (S)

Matching

A. Draw a line to match each pair of foods with the nutrient they provide:

peaches and carrots   calcium

Bran Flakes and raisins   iron

potatoes and oranges   protein

milk and yogurt   vitamin A

soybeans and eggs   vitamin C

B. Draw a line to match each nutrient with its function in the body.

vitamin A   for building and repairing body tissues

calcium   for smooth skin and gums

iron   for helping you see in the dark;
                                            for growth

protein   for building bones and teeth;
                                            for helping blood clot

vitamin C   for helping blood carry oxygen

Lesson 2
Knee Bone Connected to the . . . .

Language Arts

Interdisciplinary Emphasis

For a body to grow in length, bones need to grow and become hard. Many nutrients are needed for bone growth. Protein, vitamin C, and iron all make *collagen*; phosphorus, calcium, and vitamin A help to make bones hard.

Concepts

After viewing the demonstration, students should identify the hardening of bone as a function of calcium.

Objective

Bones are one type of living tissue in the body that require many different nutrients for growth and hardness. New bone growth begins with the formation of the protein *collagen*, which is soft and pliable. In order for bone to become hard and dense, calcium and phosphorus are deposited. These calcium and phosphorus building blocks are termed *hydroxyapatite* (hī-droxē-ap´-atīt) and the deposition of these nutrients is called *mineralization*.

Nutrition Information

Most of the absorbed calcium (99 percent) is deposited in the bones and teeth. The remaining calcium is needed to maintain its serum concentration. The ionized calcium in the serum is involved in nerve conduction, muscle contraction/relaxation and in the activation of some enzymes. The three major functions of bones are 1) to protect vital organs, 2) to give structural support and 3) to serve as a reservoir of calcium for the maintenance of the serum level of calcium.

Calcium is obtained only through absorption from dietary sources. Losses can occur through the urine and feces. The body's demand for calcium is increased during the last trimester of pregnancy and during lactation. The presence of lactose or vitamin D will increase calcium absorption. Phytic acid and oxalic acid, present in vegetables, will decrease calcium absorption by binding the mineral to form an insoluble salt. The long-term effect of an inadequate intake of calcium can lead to serious problems.

Two health conditions associated with long-term low intakes of calcium are osteoporosis and periodontal disease. Osteoporosis is defined as decreased bone density. The balance of elements found in bone is not decreased, but all components are reduced. The condition in which the balance of elements in bones is upset is called osteomalacia.

Periodontal disease refers to the disease of the supporting structures of the teeth that may result in their breaking off. Dental caries combined with periodontal disease constitutes the most prevalent dietobacterial disease in the United States.

The Recommended Dietary Allowance (RDA) of calcium for an eleven- to fourteen-year-old child is 1200 mg. The main dietary sources of calcium continue to be milk and milk products. It is difficult to obtain the recommended level of calcium if milk products are excluded from the diet. See Food Composition Table for Selected Nutrients (Appendix D) for other food sources of calcium.

Activity

Materials Needed
clean dry chicken bones
jar
white vinegar (enough to cover the chicken bones in the jar)
Bones and Growth (worksheet)

Part A
To illustrate the protein component of bone, display and demonstrate the differences between a clean, dry chicken bone and one that has been soaked in vinegar for several days. The soaked bones will be a flexible, protein material lacking the hydroxyapatite that has been dissolved away. This flexible protein is called *collagen*.

Part B
Have each student read and compare the worksheet Bones and Growth. Because the worksheet is long, you may wish to discuss the correct answers halfway through (question 17).

Answer Key to Bones and Growth
1. how long the bones grow
2. cells
3. make new bone cells
4. true
5. true
6. a builder
7. nutrients
8. collagen
9. outside the cells, forming the foundation of the bone
10. strong and flexible
11. crystals of mineral or calcium and phosphorus
12. calcium and phosphorus
13. Ca is calcium
14. P is protein
15. A is vitamin A
16. C is vitamin C
17. mineral or nutrient
18. foods rich in protein
19. the sunshine vitamin
20. sunshine helps make vitamin D
21. helps absorb more calcium from food; helps bone grow properly
22. sunshine
23. vitamin D fortified foods
24. milk
25. foundation

26. collagen
27. calcium
28. strong and rigid
29. collagen
30. lack of vitamin C
31. helps release energy from food; helps form collagen
32. true
33. true

Invite each student to write a story about Os (pronounced *oss*) and the Bone Makers. The individual stories may be used to assess each student's comprehension of the lesson.

The following ideas should be considered as inclusions to be woven into the story.
• Bones grow by becoming longer and thicker, changing shape, adding more cells, or getting harder.
• Protein and vitamin C help form collagen.
• Carbohydrate, protein, and vitamin A help in bone growth.
• Calcium, phosphorus, and vitamin D help make bone crystals.
• Bone is made of collagen.

If you do not wish to use the evaluation procedure described above, you may use the following quiz items.

___b___ 1. Which nutrient is needed to harden bone?
     a. protein
     b. calcium
     c. vitamin C
     d. fat

___a___ 2. What has to happen before bone can be hardened?
     a. The protein, collagen, must be formed.
     b. Carbohydrate must become mineral crystals.
     c. Bone cells must die.
     d. Ground substance must become collagen.

___d___ 3. If your friend Carlos said that Iron CaPAC is needed for growing bones, how should you answer him?
     a. Wrong, bones do not grow.
     b. Wrong, only calcium is needed for growing bones.
     c. Right, iron is the hard part of bone.
     d. Right, each nutrient helps bones grow.

___c___ 4. What are your bones like?
     a. They are dead.
     b. They are dry.
     c. They are full of living bone cells.
     d. They don't change after they are grown.

Books
Allison, L. 1976. *Blood and Guts, A Working Guide to Your Own Insides.* Boston: Little, Brown and Company. $3.95 (S)
Arlin, M. T. 1972. *The Science of Nutrition.* New York: MacMillan Publishing Co. $12.95 (T)
Church, C. F., and Church, H. N. 1975. *Food Values of Portions Commonly Used.* 12th ed. Philadelphia: J.B. Lippincott. $7.95 (T)
Deutsch, R. 1976. *Realities of Nutrition.* Palo Alto: Bull Publishing Co. $8.50 (T)

Guthrie, H. A. 1979. *Introductory Nutrition.* 4th ed. St. Louis: The C.V. Mosby Co. $16.95 (T)

Leverton, R. M. 1960. *Food Becomes You.* New York: Doubleday and Co. $1.25 (T)

McGill, M., and Pye, O. 1978. *The No-Nonsense Guide to Food and Nutrition.* New York: Butterick Publishing. $5.95 (T)

McWilliams, M., and Davis, L. 1977. *Food For You.* Lexington, Mass.: Ginn and Co., $5.13 (T)

Rahn, J. E. 1977. *Grocery Store Zoology.* New York: Atheneum Books. $6.95 (S)

Whitney, E., and Hamilton, M. 1977. *Understanding Nutrition.* St. Paul: West Publishing Co. $15.95 (T)

Pamphlets

"A Primer on Dietary Minerals." 1974. FDA Consumer, DHEW Publication No. (FDA) 75-2013, Government Printing Office, Superintendent of Documents, Washington, DC 20402. Free reprint. (T)

"Nutrition Source Book, 1978." National Dairy Council, 6300 N. River Road, Rosemont, IL 60018. $2 (T)

Articles

"Calcium in Bone Health." 1976. *Dairy Council Digest* 47:31–35. (T)

Lutwak, L. 1974. "Dietary Calcium and the Reversal of Bone Demineralization." *Nutrition News* 37:1–4(February). (T)

Bones and Growth

Directions: This activity is divided into frames. The frames are separated by lines that go across the page. Some frames give information. Other frames ask questions for you to answer. Answer the questions on the lines provided.

How tall a person grows depends on how long the bones grow. Did you know that bone is made of cells? The cells are like your other cells, and their special job is making new bone. For bone to grow, many bone cells are needed. Bone cells make new bone cells. More bone cells mean bigger bones. So bone growth needs more cells.

1. How tall a person grows depends on _____
   _____ .

2. Bones are made of _____
   _____ .

3. New bone is made when bone cells _____ .

All cells need nutrients to grow. Some nutrients give energy. Some nutrients become part of the cell. Bone cells need nutrients for energy. Some special nutrients are needed to make bone.

4. Bone cells need energy to make bone.
   a) true   b) false   Answer _____

5. Bone cells need special nutrients to make bones.
   a) true   b) false   Answer _____

You can think of a bone cell as a builder. A builder needs materials to build a house, a wall, or a floor. The bone cell is like a builder because it builds bone. House builders get materials from suppliers. However, bone cells make their own building materials for bone from special nutrients.

6. Bone cells are like _____ .

7. Bone cells make their own building materials from _____ .

When a builder constructs a house, he starts with a foundation. Bone cells also make a foundation called *collagen*. The cell puts collagen all around itself (outside of the cell). Collagen is a type of protein. The collagen forms long strands that are linked to each other like a net. This collagen foundation is very strong and flexible.

8. What is the foundation for bone? _____

9. The cell puts the collagen inside or outside the cell? _____

10. Write two characteristics of collagen.

_____

_____

After the foundation is made by the bone cells, mineral crystals form on the foundation. You can think of the crystals as building blocks. The building blocks are mainly calcium and phosphorus. The crystals of calcium and phosphorus "building blocks" make the bone strong and rigid.

11. What are the building blocks of bone? _____

12. Of what minerals are the building blocks made? _____

_____

Many other nutrients besides calcium and phosphorus are needed to make bone. We have learned about some of these nutrients. Do you remember Iron CaPAC and what each letter or symbol represents?

13. Ca is _____

14. P is _____

15. A is _____

16. C is _____

All of these nutrients, plus phosphorus and vitamin D, are necessary for bone to form. Protein food sources also supply phosphorus. By getting enough protein, you will get enough phosphorus.

17. Phosphorus is a _____

18. Food sources of phosphorus include _____

VITAMIN D IS MADE

Vitamin D is sometimes called the "sunshine vitamin." This is because sunshine changes a substance in your skin into vitamin D. Vitamin D helps your body absorb calcium from your food. It also helps to make bones grow properly.

19. Vitamin D is sometimes called _____

20. Why do people say that sunshine is food for you? _____

21. Vitamin D in your body helps do two things. What are they?

a. _____

b. _____

In the United States, vitamin D is added to pasteurized and homogenized milk. However, if you lived where vitamin D is not added to foods, you might not get enough from your food.

22. If you could not get enough vitamin D from your food, where else could you get it? _____

Some countries have little sunshine, and their food is not fortified with vitamin D. Children in those countries may have a deficiency disease called rickets.

23. We do not worry about getting enough vitamin D if we eat or drink what kind of foods?

_____

24. The food that is most often fortified with vitamin D is _____

A protein (P) forms the foundation of bone. The special protein is called collagen.

25. What part of the bone is protein? _____

_____

26. The protein is called _____

The Ca is necessary for the building blocks of bone. It forms a crystal with phosphorus. The crystals make the bone strong and rigid.

27. The bone crystals are made up of phosphorus and _____

28. The crystals make the bone _____

The last letter in Iron CaPAC stands for vitamin C. Vitamin C helps the cells make collagen. Collagen is part of the foundation on which bone crystals form. Many years ago, sailors used to get a disease called scurvy. They didn't have citrus fruits to eat during long journeys, so they didn't get enough vitamin C. One of the results of scurvy is improper collagen formation.

Bones and Growth (D)

29. Vitamin C is necessary for _____ formation.

30. Scurvy is caused by _____

What about iron? Iron carries oxygen to the cells. The cells use oxygen to release energy from carbohydrates. Growing bone need energy. Iron also helps form collagen.

31. In what two ways does iron help bone growth?
    _____ and _____

Children's bones increase in size. Adult bones are remolded into different shapes but don't increase in size. Both children and adults need bone-growing nutrients. Children need more calcium than adults because their bones are increasing in size.
Iron CaPAC and vitamin D are the main nutrients for proper bone formation and growth. Nutrition scientists have also found that other substances are needed in very small amounts for proper bone growth. If you eat a variety of foods you will probably get all the other nutrients needed for bone growth.

32. The bone cells increase bone size in a young person.
    a) true   b) false   Answer _____

33. Both old and young persons should have balanced diets for their bones.
    a) true   b) false   Answer _____

Lesson 3
Who's Bigger?

Language Arts/Mathematics

No two healthy people grow at the same rate. This is okay.

Students should conclude orally that there is no particular right height to be.

This lesson broadens the focus from bone growth to overall growth. The growth of individuals is dependent on what they eat as well as on genetic factors. The latter cannot be manipulated, but through a balanced diet the maximum benefits of nutrition and heredity can be obtained. The influence of heredity will be examined more closely in the next lesson.

   The nutrients involved in bone growth are also needed for the growth of other parts of the body. The exposure to Mexican foods in this lesson should broaden the student's assumptions about the nutrient-growth relationship as it pertains to other cultures. Simultaneously, the repertoire of food choices should also be expanded.

This activity will span two or more class periods.

Materials Needed
butcher paper (long roll of paper approx. 36 inches wide)
felt markers or crayons
meterstick
masking tape
Key Nutrients in Foods (Appendix A)
Sizing You Up
Mexican-American Meal
Mexican Meal Nutrient Sources

Part A
   Draw five or six horizontal lines, roughly 50 to 60 cm apart, from the bottom to the top of the blackboard. Number the lines. Ask students which line is closest to their height. Have students stay in their seats and refer to the number of the line when answering. Each student should be called in turn, and you will write their initials next to the lines they

Interdisciplinary Emphasis

Concepts

Objective

Nutrition Information

Activity

identify. Don't erase; save the estimates to compare with paper outlines later. This will reinforce metric estimating skills.

Part B

This suggestion should be made to the students: "Let's find out exactly how tall we are." Divide the class into pairs, or have them choose a partner. Push the desks aside and pass out two pieces of paper and one crayon or felt marker to each pair. Spread one piece of paper on the floor. The first student should lie down on it and have the second student trace the first as accurately as possible. Caution students to be careful not to soil clothing. Change papers and switch students. Each student should use a meterstick to measure the length (height) of his or her tracing in centimeters.

After all the students have made measurements, ask the class to tell you how tall fifth graders "should" be in centimeters. Students will probably voice their own height. Students should remember their heights in centimeters for use in Part C.

Part C

The tracings should be taped to the chalkboard with masking tape with all feet at the same level. Students should compare how close their outline is to the estimated height. You may wish to ask which outline is the "right" size to be? "Is there a right size to be?" Response desired: No, there is not a "right" size.

It is important that students focus frequently on the association between nutrients and growth. Therefore, you may wish to ask: "Does everyone need the same nutrients?" (Yes.) "Then why are some people taller than other people?" (Heredity, activity, amount of rest, and the amount of nutrients all make people different in size.) List answers for students to see.

Part D

Students should complete the worksheet Sizing You Up. The sheet functions as a convergent activity to help students 1) reaffirm that various heights are normal, 2) see how close their estimates were, 3) relate nutrient intake as one factor in growth, and 4) see that other cultures have different ways of getting appropriate nutrients.

Answer Key to Sizing You Up
1. (depends on the student)
2. (depends on the student)
3. Add the measurements of all class members together, then divide by the number of students.
4. Heredity, activity, amount of rest, and kinds of nutrients.
5. There is no correct height. Each person's height is correct. It is normal to have a variety of heights.
*6. Cartilage and bone matrix are made of protein.
   Muscles and other tissues are made of protein.
   Chemicals (enzymes) that help you convert food to tissue are made of protein.

---

*The answers to items 6–10 have not all been presented to the students at this time. Since students will be attempting to reason these answers, your list is more extensive so that you may be able to assist them in completions of the worksheet.

7. Calcium is part of bones.
   Calcium is part of teeth.
   Calcium helps your nerves coordinate activity.
   Calcium is used in cell membranes and for nerve reactions needed
   in exercise to help growth.
8. Vitamin C helps in cartilage and bone matrix growth.
   Vitamin C helps in tooth growth.
   Vitamin C helps absorption of iron and calcium.
   Vitamin C helps your cells build other body material.
9. Iron is part of blood cells.
   Iron helps blood carry oxygen needed to release energy for growing.
   Iron helps build bone matrix, cartilage, and other body materials.
10. Vitamin A helps keep skin tissue healthy.
    Vitamin A helps bone change its shape to accommodate demands
    of exercise.
    Vitamin A helps cells specialize (not directly obvious as a growth
    nutrient).
11. Phosphorus is used in bone and teeth growth.
12. Vitamin D helps you absorb calcium, which is needed in bone and
    teeth growth.

Part E
   Distribute to the students copies of the worksheets Mexican-American
Menu and Mexican Meal Nutrient Sources. Have students read these
recipes, then list food sources for the nutrients found on the worksheet.
Students should use Appendix A, Key Nutrients in Food, as a reference.
The questions given on the worksheet may also be used as part of a
class discussion.

Answer Key to Mexican-Meal Nutrient Sources
protein: ground beef, eggs, milk
calcium: milk, evaporated milk
iron: ground beef, eggs, cornmeal
vitamin A: milk, eggs, avocado
vitamin C: pepper, onion, tomatoes, lemon juice, avocado, tomato paste
To evaluate the class, use the completed worksheet, Sizing You Up.   Evaluation

Note: Please read lesson 6. Preparation of the activity must begin at this
time in order to have all materials ready for students.

Books   References
Clairborne, C. 1971. *The New York Times International Cookbook.* New   and
   York: Harper and Row Publishers. $20 (T)   Resources
Leonard, J. 1968. *Recipes—Latin American Cooking.* New York: Time-
   Life Foods of the World Books. $12.95 plus $1.63 shipping and
   handling. (S,T)
McWilliams, M. 1975. *Nutrition for the Growing Years.* 2d ed. New York:
   John Wiley and Sons. $12.50 (T)
Valadian, I., and Porter, D. 1977. *Physical Growth and Development
   from Conception to Maturity.* Boston: Little, Brown and Co. $15 (T)

Posters
Nutritional Awareness Instruction Series for Classroom Use—With
   Lesson Plans for African Foods, American Indian Foods, and
   Mexican-American Foods. 1973. *Family Circle Magazine*, 488 Madison
   Ave., NY 10022. Three posters/three lessons. $9 (S)

Sizing You Up

Name _____

1. Your estimated height was between which two lines?
   _____ cm and _____ cm

2. What was the measured height of your drawing? _____ cm

3. Write how you would find the average height of the class.

4. What causes differences in height? _____ ,
   _____ , _____ and _____ .

5. Is there a correct height for your age? _____

To answer questions 6 through 12, you will need to think about what you learned in the previous lesson.

6. How does protein help you grow? _____
   _____

7. How does calcium help you grow? _____
   _____

8. How does vitamin C help you grow? _____
   _____

9. How does iron help you grow? _____
   _____

10. How does vitamin A help you grow? _____
    _____

11. How does phosphorus help you grow? _____
    _____

12. How does vitamin D help you grow? _____
    _____

Mexican-American Menu
Tamale Pie (Serves 8)

425° F.   20 to 25 minutes

This is a hot casserole with cornbread topping spread over the top, leaving the center open.

Brown 1½ lbs. ground beef in large frypan or dutch oven with 1 Tbsp. shortening. Add and simmer for 10 minutes:

½ c. chopped onion	1 12-oz. can whole kernel corn
½ c. chopped pepper	½ c. sliced pitted olives
1 garlic clove, minced	4 t. chili powder
1 6-oz. can tomato paste	1 T. sugar
1 8-oz. can tomato sauce	½ t. salt
½ c. sugar	⅛ t. cayenne

Pour into 2½-quart greased casserole. Add cornbread topping.

Cornbread topping
Sift together:

1 c. cornmeal	2 t. baking powder
¼ c. flour	½ t. salt

Stir and mix thoroughly with above ingredients:

2 T. chopped parsley	1 egg
¾ c. milk	2 T. melted shortening

Bake.

Flan (Custard)

Serves 8 to 10

Flan is a national dessert of Mexico.

- 1¾ c. sugar
- 8 eggs
- 2 (12 to 14 oz.) cans evaporated milk
- 2 t. vanilla extract

Put 1 cup of sugar into a deep pan in which the custard is to be baked. Place over moderate heat, stirring constantly until sugar melts and turns golden. Tilt pan around until it is entirely coated with caramel. Cool while making custard. Beat eggs, add milk, remaining ¾ cup sugar, and vanilla. Mix well. Strain into caramel coated pan and place in larger pan containing hot water. Bake at 350° F. for about 1 hour or until knife inserted into the center comes out clean. Cool. Unmold onto serving platter. Cool further until serving time. Flans are best if made ahead and chilled thoroughly before serving.

Spoon into serving dishes.

Mexican-Meal Nutrient Sources

Directions: Write two good sources for each nutrient from this meal eaten by
Mexican-American boys and girls. Use Appendix A: Key Nutrients in
Foods to determine the nutrients in each food item.

Vitamin A	Vitamin C	Iron	Calcium	Protein
_____	_____	_____	_____	_____
_____	_____	_____	_____	_____

Is this menu nutritious? _____ Why do you think so? _____
_____

Is this menu nutritionally balanced? _____ Why do you think so? _____
_____
_____

Lesson 4
How Tall Is Your Family Tree?

Language Arts	Interdisciplinary Emphasis
How tall you grow depends a lot on how tall your parents and your grandparents are. Proper nutrition and keeping well help insure that you will grow the way you should.	Concepts
Students should be able to predict their adult height based on information they gather about the height of parents, grandparents, and great-grandparents.	Objective
A well-balanced diet and exercise will help maintain a person's health and well-being. No one can control genetic factors that determine an individual's adult height, but poor health and nutrition can alter a person's growth so that the expected height is not achieved.	Nutrition Information
This activity will span at least two class periods.	Activity

Materials Needed
Family Tree (worksheet)

Part A
   Hand out the worksheet Family Tree to each student. Allow the students research time to complete the chart, including their conferring with their families. If the information cannot be obtained, ask the students to list an approximate measure.

Part B
   After students have completed the take-home assignment, follow up with a discussion of the results. Relate the results to changes that may occur as a consequence of poor nutrition.
Questions for thought:
• What do you think about when you say the word *growing*? (How tall you are and how much you weigh; as you grow you get taller and heavier; it is normal to gain weight while you are growing.)
• How tall do you think you will be when you are an adult?
• What factors determine your height? (Proper nutrition, heredity, amount of rest, amount of exercise, and state of health.)

● What factors can we control to insure that we will reach the expected height? (All but heredity.)

Alternate Activity

Materials Needed
Family Tree
How Tall Will Liz Be?

Handout the reading How Tall Will Liz Be? and the worksheet Family Tree. Students should complete both the reading and the worksheet. Follow up this assignment with a discussion incorporating the same "Questions for thought" found in part B of the activity.

From the heights of grandparents and parents in the reading, students may notice the gradual increase in height from generation to generation and question you about this. You may use this opportunity to point out that health care and the nutritional quality of the diet in America has improved from generation to generation. Therefore, people are coming closer to reaching their genetic potential in height. In other words, great-grandparents and grandparents share common genetic factors (heredity) with parents and their children, but they may not have grown as tall as they could have because their diet and health may not have been of the high quality it is today. It remains to be determined whether further improvements in the overall diet and health care of Americans will result in increased height in future generations.

Answer Key to How Tall Will Liz Be?
1. Taller. Because of heredity: her parents and grandparents are taller.
2. No. Because proper exercise and a nutritious diet are important in helping you grow as tall as you should be.

Evaluation

__b__ 1. Several factors affect your growth. Of the two factors listed below, which factor is beyond your control?
   a. nutrition
   b. heredity

List some other factors besides nutrition and heredity that may affect an individual's growth.

2. _(exercise)_____

3. _(rest)_____

4. _(health)_____

References and Resources

Books
Cornacchia, H. J.; Staton, W. M.; and Irwin, L. W. 1970. *Health in Elementary Schools.* St. Louis: The C.V. Mosby Co. $12.25 (T)
Fodor, J. T.; Class, L. H.; Gmur, B. C.; Moore, V. D.; and Neilson, E. A. 1977. *Health for Living.* River Forest, Ill.: Laidlaw Brothers. $6.18 (S,T)

Booklet
EPSDT Handbook: Anthropometric Measurements. 1977. Bureau of Public Health Services, Michigan Dept. of Public Health, Baker-Olin West Building, 3500 N. Logan Street, P.O. Box 30035, Lansing, MI 48909. No. H-712-A-D. (T)

Posters
"My Growth Record." 1975. National Dairy Council No. B053, 6300 N. River Road, Rosemont, IL 60018. 5.. (S)

Family Tree

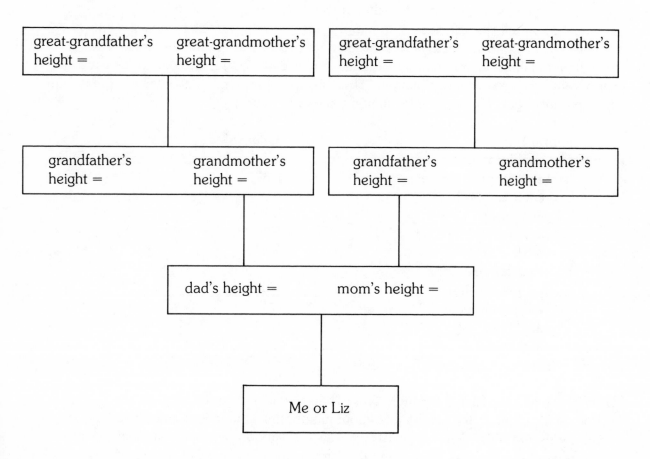

Paternal

Maternal

| great-grandfather's height = | great-grandmother's height = | great-grandfather's height = | great-grandmother's height = |

| grandfather's height = | grandmother's height = | grandfather's height = | grandmother's height = |

| dad's height = | mom's height = |

| Me or Liz |

I predict (circle one) Liz's or my height as an adult will be _____ .

How Tall Will Liz Be?

Liz is a healthy fifth-grade girl. She eats properly and sleeps nine hours every night. Every day she rides her bike, and she jogs several times a week.

Liz remembers from her health lesson in school that many things affect how tall you grow—nutrition, sleep, the state of health, exercise, and heredity. Liz has been wondering how tall she will be as an adult. Because heredity affects height, she knows that her adult height will depend on how tall her parents and grandparents are. Even the height of her great-grandparents will affect her height. So Liz decides to measure her parents' and grandparents' heights. Then she asks her parents how tall her great-grandparents were. This is the information Liz found:

Family Member	Height
Maternal (mother's side):	
great-grandfather	5'8"
great-grandmother	5'0"
grandfather	5'10"
grandmother	5'1"
mother	5'3"
Paternal (father's side):	
great-grandfather	5'9"
great-grandmother	5'1"
grandfather	5'11"
grandmother	5'4"
father	6'

Using these heights, fill in the Family Tree. Then predict Liz's adult height.

Lucy is Liz's friend. She also sleeps about nine hours a night, eats a balanced diet, and bicycles and roller skates regularly. However, Lucy's grandparents and parents are an average of three inches taller than Liz's. Which would you predict—that Lucy will have an adult height taller or shorter than Liz? (1) _____ Why? _____
_____

If Lucy continually ate poorly and got very little exercise, do you think she would grow as tall as she could? (2) _____ Why? _____
_____

Lesson 5
Energy Traps, Part I

Science	Interdisciplinary Emphasis

Our energy comes from the sun through plants and animals.

Concept

Students should be able to explain how humans obtain energy from the sun.

Objective

The direct source of energy for plants is the sun. Obviously, animals (and humans) cannot directly obtain energy from the sun but must obtain it from eating.

Nutrition Information

- Plants, utilizing the sun's energy, combine *carbon dioxide* (CO_2) and *water* (H_2O) to form *glucose* (sugar).
- Animals, directly or indirectly (through eating other animals), ingest plants.

Actually, both plants and animals can be referred to as "energy traps." The process by which plants trap energy is called *photosynthesis*:

$$\text{Sunlight} + CO_2 + H_2O \longrightarrow \text{Glucose}$$

Animals and humans have varying amounts of trapped energy, stored to a lesser degree as *glycogen* and to a greater degree as fat. Additionally, animals and humans have a large degree of protein in their muscles. Protein, as discussed in the fourth grade curriculum, can provide energy and therefore also represents a form of trapped (stored) energy. However, it is not desirable to break down muscle tissue for energy; thus we commonly do not think of muscle tissue as stored energy.

This activity will require about one hour of student time.

Activity

Materials Needed
Seeds of a fruit or vegetable and that fruit or vegetable. Suggested are one or more of the following:

pumpkin	beets (with tops)
squash	carrots (with tops)
green beans	apple

Energy Traps

Part A
  Present to the students one or more of the above plants and a seed

from each. Students should write or illustrate their ideas about how the seed became a plant—what from the environment might have been used and how. Write several of the students' ideas on the board or on a transparency and save for later.

Part B

Have students read Energy Traps, after which they should review their earlier ideas or drawings on how a seed becomes a plant and make changes or additions. Follow with a discussion in which the ideas on the board or a transparency are corrected or expanded. It is important that students emerge from this discussion with a basic understanding of the idea that "plants trap energy from the sun and use it in producing usable energy for animals and humans."

Part C

To illustrate to the students how animal foods they eat are also "energy traps," ask students: 1) How do cattle, chickens, hogs, fish, and other animals trap energy, and what happens to that trapped energy? 2) How do children trap energy, and what happens to that energy? Important points to discuss here are as follows:

• Animals that we eat trap energy mostly through eating plant foods (although some animals, such as hogs, do eat fishmeal; some fish also eat other fish.)

• This energy the animal has trapped helps him grow. The excess is stored as fat. Some animals (chickens and cows) also use the trapped energy to make other foods (eggs and milk.)

• Children trap energy when they eat either plants or animals. Children use this energy to grow. Excess energy is stored as fat.

Evaluation

  c   1. From where does a chicken get its energy?
     a. The sun's rays enter the chicken's feathers.
     b. A chicken makes its own energy from water and carbon dioxide.
     c. A chicken eats stored energy in plants.
     d. All of its energy comes from the egg.

  a   2. Where does a plant get its energy?
     a. The plant's leaves absorb energy from the sun's rays.
     b. The plant makes energy from fertilizer.
     c. The plant eats soil.
     d. The plant eats other plants after it chokes them.

  d   3. Tigers are meat eaters. Where does a tiger get its energy?
     a. A tiger's fur absorbs energy from the sun's rays.
     b. A tiger makes energy from the air.
     c. A tiger eats energy stored in plants.
     d. A tiger eats energy stored in other animals.

  b   4. Suppose you had to quit eating all meat. What would happen to you?
     a. You could get your energy from sun tanning.
     b. You could get your energy from the plants you eat.
     c. You could make your energy from carbon dioxide and water.
     d. You would die.

__b__ 5. Which substance supplies energy for humans?
   a. air
   b. plants
   c. water
   d. all of the above

Books

Cobb, V., and Lippman, P. 1972. *Science Experiments You Can Eat.* Philadelphia: J. B. Lippincott Co. $4.95 (S)

Ford, J. M., and Monroe, J. E. 1977. *Living Systems: Principles and Relationships.* 3rd ed. San Francisco: Canfield Press. $16.95 (T)

Navarra, J. G., and Zafforoni, J. 1971. *The Young Scientist: His Experiments and Hypothesis.* New York: Harper and Row. $7.50 (S,T)

Films/Filmstrips

Food, Energy, and You. 1978. Perennial Education, Inc., 477 Roger Williams P.O. Box 855, Ravinia, Highland Park, IL 60035. Film, 16mm, color, sound, 19 minutes, study guide $295/rental $29.50 (S)

References and Resources

Energy Traps

Have you ever wondered how people catch energy? You know that you need energy to play soccer, use a skate board, strum a guitar, or turn the pages in a book. But how do you capture the energy in the first place?

Would you be able to capture energy with a butterfly net? After you quit laughing, what about a bucket? What about a glass box?

Sunlight gives energy, but it has to be caught. If you put a bucket of ice in the sunshine, what happens to the ice?

Water captures light energy from the sun and becomes warmer. Thus, the light energy has become heat energy. When things get warmer, they have gained heat energy. One way we can tell if energy is trapped is by taking the temperature of the energy trap.

In the same manner, air in a closed glass container can capture sunlight. It becomes warm air. You may have a terrarium or a greenhouse that has sun-warmed air. But we need energy, too. We don't get any energy from eating air! We can drink warm water, but that doesn't give us usable energy either. Something else must capture energy for us. The next three paragraphs describe an experiment involving another kind of energy trap.

van Helmont's Experiment

Somewhat ahead of his time, Jean-Baptiste van Helmont had an interesting idea.[*] He thought that you could find out about things better by making measurements and observations than by just studying about them in books. Van Helmont was a physician and scientist during the time when most people thought true science was what Aristotle wrote. This was about 1600 A.D.

Van Helmont's beautiful and simple experiment was to weigh a small willow shoot and a tub of soil. He planted the shoot in the tub of soil. For five years he just watered it. Then he removed the tree and weighed it. It weighed 164 pounds. The soil weighed a few ounces less than it did five years previously.

He concluded that the extra weight of the tree had come from the water. Like many scientific conclusions, it was partly right and partly wrong. We now know that much of the weight of the tree came from carbon dioxide. Carbon dioxide is what you exhale. In van Helmont's time, no one knew that carbon dioxide even existed. This experiment gave us the beginning of our knowledge of photosynthesis.

[*]From *This Is Life: Essays in Modern Biology*, edited by Willis H. Johnson and William C. Steere. Copyright 1962 by Holt, Rinehart and Winston. Reprinted by permission of Holt, Rinehart and Winston.

Now, let us look at a word. The word is *photosynthesis*. Photosynthesis is what enabled van Helmont's willow tree to grow and grow. Photosynthesis is a long word, but it contains several shorter word roots. *Photo* is something you have seen before. Photo is the Greek root word that means *light*. In a photograph, light is captured by chemicals on the film to make an image. A photograph is an energy trap too.

Synthesis comes from the Greek root word that means "put things together." You could also consider building something as synthesis. Synthetic fabrics are man-made fabrics. People put chemicals together to make the fabrics.

Photosynthesis means that light caused something to be put together. Sunlight causes plants to put carbon dioxide and water together to make sugar. The plant captures the sunlight for energy. The plant is an energy trap! The energy makes the chemicals come together and become something else. Carbon dioxide and water become sugar in the plant. The plant changes sugar to starch. For example, corn on the cob will taste sweeter if it is picked and eaten early in the corn season. Corn eaten late in the season will not taste as sweet because some of the sugar has been changed to starch.

Now, return to your sheet of paper where you wrote down or drew how a seed becomes a plant. Would you add or change anything? If "yes," make the additions and changes. You'll be given a chance to share your work with the class.

Lesson 6
Energy Traps, Part II

Science/Mathematics   Interdisciplinary Emphasis

Energy-storing chemicals in our food are the three nutrients: Concept
carbohydrates, fats, and proteins.

Students should be able to identify how many energy-supplying nutrients   Objective
there are and name them.

The three nutrients that provide energy in our diets are carbohydrate, fat,   Nutrition Information
and protein. Alcohol also provides energy, but this will not be addressed
here. Carbohydrates and fats are the preferred fuel nutrients for our
body, but protein is also used for energy if it is eaten in quantities greater
than are needed for tissue growth, maintenance, and repair (and
Americans, characteristically, do eat more protein than is needed for
these processes).
   Plants store most of their energy as carbohydrate (sugar and starch).
Interestingly, some plant parts are richer in starch than others. For
example, tubers, roots, and seeds have more starch than leaves or stems.
However, some plant foods do have a considerable amount of fat,
including all nuts, sunflower seeds, sesame seeds, soybeans, avocados,
and olives. Additionally, some plant foods are good protein sources,
including legumes (peanuts, soybeans, and other dried beans and peas),
several types of nuts, sunflower seeds, and sesame seeds. Grains also
provide some protein but in lesser amounts.
   Animals store very little energy in the form of carbohydrate (glycogen
or "animal starch"). Fat and protein provide most of the energy we
derive from eating flesh foods and other animal products (milk is an
exception to this rule, providing a considerable amount of carbohydrate).
   This lesson's activity reinforces the concept from the last lesson, again
illustrating that plants and animals are "energy traps." Furthermore, it
points out the three energy-contributing nutrients and the extent to which
they are present in various plant and animal foods.

Preparation of this activity must begin three to four weeks ahead of time   Activity
if you and the students are going to grow the plants to be used. The
activity requires from one to 1½ hours of student time.

Materials Needed

Amounts of the following articles will depend on whether students work in groups or you demonstrate:

   bean seeds (*Phaiseolus vulgaris*)
   bean plants (grown three to four weeks ahead of time)
   empty quart or half-gallon milk cartons displaying a nutrient label
      (must be *whole* milk)
   paper towels
   iodine solution with dropper
   hot plate
   tongs or pot holder
   Bean-Green Investigation
   Self-Check Answer Key

The activity is set up for students to work in groups, following the Bean-Green Investigation worksheet. Since bean plants are necessary for the Bean-Green Investigation, they will have to grow their plants (as they are directed on the Bean-Green Investigation worksheet steps 1.1 and 1.2) three to four weeks ahead of time. An alternative to group work is your demonstration of steps outlined in the worksheet, the students answering the worksheet questions as you go along. (Obviously, you will need a couple of bean plants if you choose this route.) An alternative to your growing the plants is purchasing them from your local greenhouse. (Note: The common bean plant is given the technical name *Phaiseolus vulgaris*, "vulgaris" meaning common.)

If you do decide to have the students work in groups, give instructions for handling the iodine solution so that it does not stain skin or clothing.

Regardless of whether you choose to have the students work in groups, you will need to prepare leaves for the starch test by 1) boiling them for five minutes in water; 2) boiling them in rubbing alcohol or ditto fluid for about two minutes over a hot plate (Alcohol fumes are combustible, and care should be used. A larger container placed upside down over the boiler will extinguish flames), and 3) cooling leaves and distributing them, if you work in groups.

Alternate Activity

Materials Needed

An empty package or container, each having a nutrient label, of the following foods:

   whole milk
   tuna fish (or other canned fish)
   cheese (any type except cottage or ricotta)
   canned meat (You may want to include a couple of varieties, such as
      sausage, chicken, weiners, spam, or other.)
   Rice Krispies or Corn Flakes
   fruit juice
   peanuts (or some type of nut)
   canned corn (whole kernel)
   canned fruit (pineapple, peaches, or applesauce) or dried fruit (raisins,
      dates, or apples)
   sunflower seeds (or sesame seeds or soybeans)

This activity does not directly reinforce the concept presented in the previous lesson, but it does fully develop this lesson's concept. This activity is interdisciplinary with mathematics, involving the calculation of percentages. (If percentages have not yet been introduced, you may wish to have students give answers in fractions instead.)

You will need to set up the foods listed under Materials Needed on a table where students can conveniently view them. You may also wish to construct a form for students to use in Part A.

Part A

Divide students into pairs. One student of each pair should answer the four questions below for *each* animal food. The other student should answer the four questions below for *each* plant food. Each pair should then compare and discuss their answers, using their answers to identify commonalities and differences between the plant and animal foods.

1) Which nutrients supply energy (Calories)?
2) How much energy is there in one serving of this food?
3) What is the total weight, in grams, of the protein, carbohydrate, and fat in this food?
4) Out of the total weight calculated in step 3, what is the percentage (or fraction) of the weight that comes from:
   a) protein?
   b) carbohydrate?
   c) fat?

Part B

After students have finished comparing and discussing their answers, discuss with students any observations they have. The following conclusions should be drawn:

1) Fats, carbohydrates, and proteins are the three energy-supplying nutrients.
2) All foods from plants give us carbohydrate. In fact, the greater number of Calories in many plant foods come from carbohydrate.
3) Some plant foods also have quite a bit of fat and/or protein.
4) Most foods that come from animals do not give us carbohydrate. Exceptions are milk, yogurt, and ice cream.
5) The Calories in most animal foods come from fat and/or protein.

__d__ 1. How many nutrients supply energy?   Evaluation
         a. 1
         b. 2
         c. 6
         d. 3
         e. 0
__b__ 2. Which of the following choices lists *only* nutrients that supply energy?
         a. fats and water
         b. protein and fat
         c. minerals, water, and carbohydrate
         d. vitamins and minerals
         e. water and carbohydrate
__c__ 3. One energy-supplying nutrient that all plant foods have is:
         a. vitamin A
         b. iron
         c. carbohydrate
         d. water
         e. fat

References
and
Resources

Books

Cobb, V., and Lippman, P. 1972. *Science Experiments You Can Eat.* Philadelphia: J. B. Lippincott Co. $4.95 (S)

Labuza, T. P., and Sloan, A. E. 1977. *Food for Thought.* 2d ed. Westport, Conn.: The AVI Publishing Co. $7.50 (T)

Pamphlets

"A Primer on Four Nutrients: Proteins, Carbohydrates, Fats and Fiber." 1975. *FDA Consumer,* DHEW Publication No. (FDA) 75-2026, Government Printing Office, Superintendent of Documents, Washington, DC 20402. Free reprint. (T)

"Food Is More Than Just Something to Eat." 1977. U.S. Dept. of Health, Education, and Welfare, Public Health Service, Food and Drug Administration, 5600 Fishers Lane, Rockville, MD 20852. Free. (T)

Films/Filmstrips

Food, Energy, and You. 1978. Perennial Education, Inc., 477 Roger Williams, P.O. Box 855, Ravinia, Highland Park, IL 60035. Film, 16mm, color, sound, 19 minutes, study guide. $295/rental $29.50 (S)

"How Food Affects You." 1963. U.S. Extension Service, Washington, DC 20250. Filmstrip/teacher's guide and narration. $11 (S)

"How Food Becomes You." 1964. National Dairy Council, 6300 N. River Road, Rosemont, IL 60018. Filmstrip, script, 15 minutes. $5 (S)

Bean-Green Investigation

Step 1   1.1   With three other students, obtain 20 seeds from your teacher and 4 milk cartons from the lunchroom. Cut off the top of each carton and place soil 4 centimeters deep into your carton. Add about 125 milligrams of water or until the soil is moist but not wet. Plant 5 seeds per carton about 1 centimeter from the top of the soil. Label your cartons with your initials.

1.2   Water your bean seeds 2 to 3 times per week. Let the plants grow about 3 to 4 weeks near the window. Observe plants daily.

1.3   Remove the bean plants from one carton by tearing down two sides of the carton. Gently tease the plant roots away from the soil, one plant at a time. Gently shake the soil.

1.4   While the bean seed grew to the bean plant, did it lose or gain energy? _____

Step 2   2.1   Test a soaked bean seed for starch. Cut the seed in half and drop some iodine solution on it. Iodine solution turns blue or purple when it touches starch. Did it turn dark purple? _____

2.2   Does the bean have starch in it? _____

2.3   *Suppose* you were to chew the bean for a long time. Then *suppose* you tested it again with iodine. What color would it be? _____ (*Don't chew bean seeds!* They have poisons on them! You could try it with dried navy beans, however.)

Step 3   3.1   Test some bean plant stems for starch. Mash the stems on a paper towel. Drop iodine solution on the mashed stems. What color did the iodine become? _____

3.2   Is there as much starch in the stem as in the seed? _____

Step 4   4.1   Test some bean plant leaves for starch. Use leaves your teacher has boiled for you. They will not be bright green. Place a leaf on a paper towel. Drop two drops of iodine on it. What color does the iodine become? _____

4.2   Does the leaf have as much starch as the bean? _____

4.3   Does the leaf have as much starch as the stem? _____

4.4   Carbon dioxide is a gas. Water is a liquid or a gas. Is starch a liquid or a gas? _____

4.5   Is starch something different from carbon dioxide and water? _____

4.6   Does the plant contain energy? _____

4.7   Can you eat starch in leaves or stems or seeds? _____

4.8   Can your body break starch into nutrients? _____

4.9   Can chickens eat seeds? _____

4.10   Are beans seeds? _____

4.11   Can beef cattle eat stems and leaves? _____

4.12 Can people eat other kinds of stem and leaf foods? _____ Is Mother Nature's energy trap any good to you? (Only if you can get the energy from the energy trap for your own use.) You can eat the starch from plants. You can also eat animals that have eaten plants. Animals store energy as carbohydrate, fat, and protein. These three nutrients are made from chemicals. These three chemical compounds are the energy-providing nutrients.

Step 5   5.1 Look at a food label from whole milk. Can you distinguish the energy-providing nutrients from the rest of the nutrients on a label? _____
_____

5.2 Are the energy-providing nutrients shown on the label as grams or percentages? _____

5.3 How much energy do the three energy-providing nutrients together supply in each serving of this food? _____
_____

5.4 If you drank all the milk in the container, how much energy would you get? _____
_____

5.5 You get energy from eating plants. Much of the energy you get from plants is from carbohydrates. Plants store most of their energy as carbohydrate. However, some foods that come from plants do contribute quite a bit of energy as fat. Can you think of some examples? a) _____
_____

Some plant foods also have quite a bit of protein. Do you know of some? b) _____
_____

5.6 You get energy from eating animals that have eaten plants. Chickens are good examples. You also get energy from eating animals that eat other animals. Can you think of an animal you might eat that eats other animals? a) _____
_____

Which of the "energy" nutrients are most present in animals or foods that animals produce? b) _____
_____

5.7 But where did all this energy originally come from? _____
_____

Self-Check Answer Key

Bean-Green Experiment

1.4	It gained energy because it contained more after it grew.
2.1	yes
2.2	yes
2.3	lighter purple or brown
3.1	lighter purple
3.2	not as much
4.1	purple
4.2	not quite as much
4.3	more
4.4	no
4.5	yes
4.6	yes
4.7	yes
4.8	yes
4.9	yes
4.10	yes
4.11	yes
4.12	yes
5.1	yes. (They are above the statement "Percent of the U.S. Recommended Dietary Allowances.")
5.2	grams
5.3	Read the Calories per serving.
5.4	Multiply the number of Calories per serving times the total number of servings.
5.5	a) peanuts, nuts, and sunflower seeds
	b) kidney beans, navy beans, and peanuts
5.6	a) Bass fish eat smaller fish. Hogs eat fishmeal.
	b) Fats and proteins. (Milk is an exception. It also has carbohydrate.)
5.7	The sun

Lesson 7
How Does Your Body Get Energy?

Science

Enzymes are special chemicals in our body to help us get the energy out of fat, carbohydrate, and protein.

Students should define what enzymes are and explain how they help get the energy out of fats, carbohydrates, and protein.

In the fourth-grade curriculum (Lessons 23, 24, and 25), the processes of digestion and absorption were explained. Digestive juices, composed of specialized *enzymes*, were defined as playing a crucial role in chemical digestion. These enzymes help break down fats, carbohydrates, and proteins into absorbable forms (into *fatty acids, glucose,* and *amino acids,* in that order). The nutrients must be broken down further before energy is liberated from them. This further breakdown occurs after the nutrients have been transported to and have entered body cells. Again, enzymes play a crucial role within the cell in the further breakdown of fatty acids, glucose, and amino acids. Here, a series of chemical reactions convert the amino acids, glucose, and fatty acids into energy bundles, called ATP's (bundles of *adenosine triphosphate*). Enzymes both direct and accelerate the formation of these energy bundles.

Materials Needed
reconstituted nonfat dry milk or skimmed milk (2 cups)
two clear glasses
vinegar (2 to 3 ounces)

In the fourth-grade curriculum (Lesson 25) students learned how digestive juices were involved in the chemical breakdown of food. Since enzymes are a principle component of digestive juice, a brief review of the term *digestive juice* and its function would help set the stage for this activity.

Part A
On the board, put the word *enzyme* along with the lesson concept. Explain to students that digestive juice in the small intestine is made up of enzymes that break down fat, carbohydrate, and protein into

Interdisciplinary Emphasis

Concept

Objective

Nutrition Information

Activity

substances that can be absorbed into the blood and transported to the cells. These substances are fatty acids, glucose, and amino acids. Once these nutrients get into the cells, enzymes help break them down further so that we can obtain energy from them. (Note: You may wish to draw a diagram illustrating nutrient breakdown in the small intestine, transportation to the cells, and further breakdown in the cells.)

Part B

To illustrate the concept of enzymes breaking down nutrients, show students how vinegar causes reconstituted nonfat dry milk or skimmed milk to break apart into small pieces (coagulate and separate) almost instantaneously. Draw an analogy between this reaction and the action of enzymes on fatty acids, glucose, and amino acids in our cells: enzymes help break down these substances to yield energy, and they cause it to happen quickly.

The idea of souring milk could also be used as an analogy to help explain enzymatic action. It takes two weeks for milk to sour at refrigerator temperatures, but only several hours for it to sour in a warm room (depending on the freshness of the milk and how warm the room is). The warm air *catalyzes* (accelerates) the souring of milk just as enzymes catalyze the breakdown of fatty acids, glucose, and amino acids.

Evaluation

Based on the illustrations and explanations given, students should, in their own words, define *enzyme* and explain what enzymes do to energy—supplying nutrients. Students should be encouraged to use examples from everyday life as well as drawings in their definition and explanation.

Two sample quiz items are also given here.

__d__ 1. What do enzymes do to fats, carbohydrates, and protein?
      a. slow them down
      b. nothing
      c. dissolve them
      d. help break them up

__c__ 2. Enzymes help our bodies
      a. digest vitamins
      b. break down minerals
      c. get energy out of food
      d. make minerals

References and Resources

Books

Guyton, A. C. 1979. *Physiology of the Human Body.* 5th ed. Philadelphia: W. B. Saunders Co. $14.95 (T)

Lamb, L. E. 1974. *Metabolics: Putting Your Food Energy to Work.* New York: Harper and Row. $10.95 (T)

O'Connell, L.; Rye, J.; and Bell, P. 1981. *Nutrition in a Changing World: A Curriculum for Grade Four.* Provo, Utah: Brigham Young University Press. (T)

Films/Filmstrips

Food, Energy, and You. 1978. Perennial Education, 477 Roger Williams, P.O. Box 855, Ravinia, Highland Park, IL 60035. Film, 16mm, color, sound, 19 minutes, study guide. $295/rental $29.50 (S)

How Food Becomes Part of You. 1976. Guidance Associates, Communication Park, Box 300, White Plains, NY 10602. Filmstrip/audiocassette, 14 minutes. $39.50 (S)

Lesson 8
Putting Food Energy to Work: Part I

Health	Interdisciplinary Emphasis
The body uses food energy for many basic processes such as breathing and keeping body cells alive. These basic processes are called basal metabolism.	Concepts
We also use energy to digest and absorb food. However, digestion and absorption are not part of basal metabolism.	

Students should be able to define and identify processes that are a part of basal metabolism.

Objective

The body utilizes food energy for:
1) basic internal body processes, such as breathing, maintaining body temperature, and growth/repair of body tissue;
2) digesting and absorbing food; and
3) physical activity.

Nutrition Information

This lesson will focus only on energy requirements for basic internal body processes, collectively referred to as *basal metabolism*.

Most accurately, basal metabolism is defined as: that amount of energy utilized to sustain life while the body is at complete rest.

In the moderately active individual, about one-half of the energy expended is used in basal metabolism. This is not surprising when you realize internal organs are working around the clock, some more intensively than others. The brain and liver together consume about 50 percent of all the energy expended in basal metabolism. The kidneys, heart, and lungs also work at a fairly high rate. In addition to maintenance of body temperature and the work of body organs, other processes categorized under basal metabolism include glandular activity; muscle tonus; and synthesis of bones, teeth, muscle, and body compounds—such as hemoglobin and a variety of enzymes. (Interestingly, digestion and absorption of food is not considered to be part of basal metabolism because it occurs in a canal separate from the rest of the internal body. See Grade Four curriculum, Lesson 21.)

While, in general, the number of Calories used for basal metabolism is relatively fixed, some factors modify (to some extent) the total number of Calories used in basal metabolism.

Some of these factors are identified and explained as follows:

1) Body size: A larger body has more tissue to maintain; therefore the number of Calories required for basal metabolism is increased.
2) Body composition: Individuals with more muscle (lean body mass) require more Calories for basal metabolism.
3) Sex: Because the average male has more lean body mass than the average female, males require a greater number of Calories for basal metabolism.
4) Thyroid Secretion: An overactive or underactive thyroid gland will appreciably increase or decrease Caloric requirements for basal metabolism, respectively.

Activity

Materials Needed
Human Energy Unit Model (Appendix E)
The Digestive System (Appendix F)

Part A
Either on a transparency or on the blackboard, draw the human body as depicted in the Human Energy Unit Model (Appendix E) but do not draw in the body functions and related numbers (listed on the right) or the parallel lines. While looking at this illustration, each student should write down processes (excluding digestion and absorption of food) in his or her body that continue to occur while he or she is lying down at rest. Following this, students should volunteer their answers while you list them on or beside the drawing of the human body.

Any of the body functions on the model illustration (except digestion and absorption of food and muscle movement) not volunteered by the students should be added and explained. Pose the question "What would happen to the body if these processes stopped?" Acceptable responses would relate to eventual death. Explain that these processes are vital or basic to life and that therefore they are collectively referred to as basal metabolism.

Part B
Referring to the processes you have listed on or beside the drawing of the human body, ask students what these processes all have in common (other than the fact that they are vital to life). Acceptable responses would indicate that all these basic processes happen inside the body; therefore they are referred to as "internal." Point out that digestion and absorption of food does happen inside the body but inside a canal that is separated from the rest of the body. Therefore digestion and absorption are *not* part of basal metabolism. (Referring to the concepts and diagram of the alimentary canal in the fourth-grade curriculum, Lesson 21, would be helpful, if not essential, in developing this idea. Therefore, a diagram of the digestive system has been included in this booklet, Appendix F).

Evaluation

Listed below are five processes. If the process is a part of basal metabolism, mark "A" in the blank beside the process. If the process is *not* a part of basal metabolism, mark "B."

  B   1. digesting food
  A   2. waste removal
  A   3. breathing
  B   4. writing
  A   5. growth of bones

50

  c   6. What is the best definition of basal metabolism?
   a. the digestion of food
   b. external body processes
   c. internal body processes that keep us alive
   d. exercise needed for health

Books

Guthrie, H. A. 1979. *Introductory Nutrition.* 4th ed. St. Louis: The C.V. Mosby Co. $16.95 (T)

O'Connell, L.; Rye, J.; and Bell, P. 1981. *Nutrition in a Changing World: A Curriculum for Grade Four.* Provo, Utah: Brigham Young University Press. (T)

Articles

Mayer, J. 1966. "Why People Get Hungry." *Nutrition Today* 1:2–8 (June). (T)

Young, V. R., and Scrimshaw, N. S. 1971. "The Physiology of Starvation." *Scientific American* 225:14–21 (October). (T)

References
and
Resources

Lesson 9
Putting Food Energy to Work:
Part II

| Mathematics/Health | Interdisciplinary Emphasis |

In addition to basal metabolism, digestion, and absorption, our bodies use energy to move muscles. Muscle movement is referred to as physical activity.

Over a twenty-four-hour period, the body usually uses more energy for basal metabolism than for physical activity.

Concepts

After playing The Energy Game, each student should be able to
1) identify the three categories of energy expenditure as
   a) basal metabolism,
   b) physical activity, and
   c) digestion and absorption of food.
2) explain why the body usually uses more energy for basal metabolism than for physical activity over a twenty-four hour period.

Objective

As specified in the last lesson, the total energy needs of the body can be separated into three categories: 1) basal metabolism, 2) physical activity, and 3) digestion and absorption of food.

Nutrition Information

In the moderately active individual, approximately 50 percent of the total energy utilized over a twenty-four-hour period is used to fuel the basic metabolic processes. Of the remaining 50 percent, approximately 40 percent is consumed by physical activity and 10 percent for digestion and absorption of food. Obviously, in a sedentary person, greater than 50 percent of the total energy utilized would be for basal metabolism and in a very active person less than 50 percent would be for basal metabolism. To illustrate the latter, the daily energy needs of two males of the same age (35 years), weight (60 kg or 133 lbs.), and height (1.73 meters or 5'9"), are shown below. Note that male A is only slightly active whereas male B is quite active.

| Male A | | | Male B | | |
Activity	Time (hrs)	Calories Expended	Activity	Time (hrs)	Calories Expended
Dressing	1.0	42	Dressing	1.0	42
Sitting	8.0	192	Sitting	7.0	168

53

Walking (3mph)	2.0	240	Walking (3mph)	2.5	300	
Standing	1.0	30	Standing	1.0	30	
Typing	2.0	120	Bicycling (moderately)	2.0	300	
Dishwashing	1.0	60	Dancing	2.0	360	
Sleeping	9.0	—	Swimming (2mph)	.5	225	
			Sleeping	8.0	—	

	Male A	Male B
Total energy cost of activity for 24 hours	684	1425
Energy cost of *basal metabolism for 24 hours	1440	1440
Energy cost to digest and absorb food over 24 hours	212	286
Total daily energy cost	2336	3151
Percentage of energy used for basal metabolism	62%	46%

*Basal metabolism is calculated as follows:
1 Calorie × Body Weight (in Kilograms) × 24 hours

More detail on the energy cost of specific activities will be included in the next lesson. In this lesson's activity, all physical activity is collectively referred to as muscle movement.

Activity

Materials Needed
Human Energy Unit Model (Appendix E)
Energy Unit Master
Energy Game Board
playing pieces for Energy Game
dice for Energy Game

This activity will enable students to visualize why the body usually requires more energy for basal metabolic processes than for physical activity over a twenty-four hour period.

Part A
Review with students processes that would be categorized under basal metabolism and those that would fit under physical activity. Make sure to clarify that all voluntary muscle movement fits under physical activity, such as typing, dishwashing, running, and writing. Even sitting and standing, because of the muscles used to hold you in these positions, are categorized under physical activity.
Review that digestion and absorption of food is a separate category of energy expenditure.

Part B
Students play the Energy Game. Duplicate six Human Energy Unit (person) models. Parts should be cut as designated. All parts for each "person" should be paper-clipped together. The Energy Game Board

should be glued to a cardboard backing and laminated in plastic if your school has the facilities. Energy Units (from the Energy Unit Master) should be duplicated and cut into cards (duplicate two masters per game board). The cards should be shuffled and stacked on the game board. Six playing pieces should be accumulated. Different kinds of seeds work well. Obtain two dice. Select the first set of players, who may then read the rules and play the Energy Game.

Four to six players may play the game at one time. The goal is to collect a complete set of body cards, representing the major energy requirements of the body. The first person to do so wins.

In order to acquire each of the parts of the body, players have to both land on the appropriate space on the game board and have enough energy units to pay for the part. Body building requires both materials and energy. Body parts also need maintenance energy.

Rules of the Energy Game.
1. The starting place on the playing board is designated: the right side of the Meal Space located in the left-hand corner of the board.
2. During a turn, the player rolls the two dice.
3. The player moves the piece the number of spaces indicated by the dice. A player's choice of moves may be limited because he may not stop on a space that is already occupied.
4. The spaces have different messages:
   a) If an individual lands on Meal Space, he or she takes the top card from the Energy Unit Deck (this is the *only* way energy units are accumulated). Energy units are saved until they are needed to purchase a part of the Human Energy Unit Model.
   b) If an individual lands on a part of the Human Energy Unit Model, he or she may purchase that part if he or she has the required energy units (the player must have the exact combination of energy units to purchase a part of the model; that is, if a player has only 5- and 2-energy unit cards, that player cannot purchase a model part that requires 6 energy units; a player having only 5s and 10s cannot purchase a model part that requires 2 units.
Note: Spaces on the Energy Game Board:
   a) bold letters indicate basal metabolic functions;
   b) bold, italic letters indicate physical activity;
   c) regular letters indicate digestion; and
   d) italics indicate meal spaces.
5. Players should continue around the board until someone obtains *all* the model parts for the Human Energy Unit Model. This player is the winner.

After everyone has played the game, discuss with students any observations they have made about how much energy is required for each of the three categories of energy expenditure. Point out that the sum of all energy units on the Human Energy Unit Model is 100: 50 for basal metabolic processes, 40 for physical activity, and 10 for digestion and absorption of food. The human body usually uses as much or more energy for basal metabolism than for physical activity.

Materials Needed
Human Energy Unit Model (Appendix E)
stethoscope (optional)

Alternate Activity

Part A

Reproduce and distribute a copy of the Human Energy Unit Model to each student. Review with students the processes that are a part of basal metabolism. Students should also cite examples of processes that would be categorized under muscle movement. A more appropriate term for muscle movement is physical activity. Emphasize that digestion and absorption of food are not parts of basal metabolism or physical activity but do require energy. If students have trouble understanding why digestion and absorption require energy, you might talk about how the food gets from the mouth to the small intestine. You might also use a stethoscope, letting students listen to their stomachs churning food after lunch.

Part B

Student should sum all the energy units represented beside each process. The total will come to 100, and this figure represents the total energy needs of the day. Then students should determine the *fraction or percentage* of energy used for:

    1) all basal metabolic processes
    2) digestion and absorption of food
    3) physical activity (muscle movement)

Students should conclude that more energy is required for basal metabolism than for physical activity. A discussion should follow, highlighting why this is true (refer to the nutrition information in the previous lesson for background if necessary).

Evaluation

In blanks 1 through 3 below, write the three major ways our body uses energy.

1.   (for basal metabolism)
2.   (for digesting and absorbing food)
3.   (for physical activity)
4. The body usually uses more energy for basal metabolism than for physical activity because: (circle the correct answer)
    a. "standing" takes a lot of energy
    b. basal metabolism stops when we sleep
    c. digesting and absorbing food takes a lot of energy
    (d.) many parts inside our bodies need quite a bit of energy twenty-four hours a day.

References and Resources

Books

Mahoney, M. J., and Mahoney, K. 1976. *Permanent Weight Control.* New York: W.W. Norton and Co. $8.95 (T)

Stunkard, A. J. 1976. *The Pain of Obesity.* Palo Alto: Bull Publishing Co. $7.95 (T)

Posters

"Nutrition Sports Mobile." 1977. Sunkist Growers, Consumer Services Dept., Box 7888, Van Nuys, CA 91409. Free. (S)

Films/Filmstrips

Too Much of a Good Thing? No date (ca. 1974). March Film Enterprises, P.O. Box 8082, Shawnee Mission, KS 66208. Filmstrip/audiocassette, 17 minutes, teaching guide. $22.50 (S)

Energy Game Board

Digestion and Absorption (10)

Waste Removal (10)

Muscles for Movement (40)

Meal Space

Making Bones and Teeth (2)

Breathing (6)

Brain (15)

Making Hemoglobin (2)

Liver Working (10)

Meal Space

Heart Pumping Blood (5)

Meal Space

Energy Unit Deck

Liver Working (10)

Brain (20)

Making Hemoglobin (2)

Digestion and Absorption (10)

Waste Removal (10)

Meal Space

Start

Making Bones and Teeth (2)

Breathing (6)

1 Energy Units 1 / 1 ... 1	2 Energy Units 2 / 2 ... 2	5 Energy Units 5 / 5 ... 5	10 Energy Units 10 / 10 ... 10

1 Energy Units 1	2 Energy Units 2	5 Energy Units 5	10 Energy Units 10
1 1	2 2	5 5	10 10
1 Energy Units 1	2 Energy Units 2	5 Energy Units 5	10 Energy Units 10
1 1	2 2	5 5	10 10
1 Energy Units 1	2 Energy Units 2	5 Energy Units 5	10 Energy Units 10
1 1	2 2	5 5	10 10
1 Energy Units 1	2 Energy Units 2	5 Energy Units 5	10 Energy Units 10
1 1	2 2	5 5	10 10
1 Energy Units 1	2 Energy Units 2	5 Energy Units 5	10 Energy Units 10
1 1	2 2	5 5	10 10
1 Energy Units 1	2 Energy Units 2	5 Energy Units 5	10 Energy Units 10
1 1	2 2	5 5	10 10
1 Energy Units 1	2 Energy Units 2	5 Energy Units 5	10 Energy Units 10
1 1	2 2	5 5	10 10
1 Energy Units 1	2 Energy Units 2	5 Energy Units 5	10 Energy Units 10
1 1	2 2	5 5	10 10

Lesson 10
All about Calories

Health

Calories are the units we use to measure the amount of energy in foods. The only nutrients that supply Calories are carbohydrates, fats, and protein.

Concepts

Students should identify the three nutrients that contribute Calories to the diet.

Objective

The body needs energy for everything from climbing trees to digesting food and releasing energy itself. The *energy* the body uses comes from the nutrients *carbohydrate, protein,* and *fat* in foods and beverages. *Vitamins, minerals,* and *water* all play a role in helping us get the energy out of food, but they do not directly supply any energy. Although alcohol found in foods and beverages can be converted into energy by the body, it is not considered a nutrient. Discussion of alcohol has been omitted from this lesson. Fat contains 2¼ times as much energy as equivalent weights of carbohydrate or protein (alcohol supplies seven Calories per gram).

Nutrition Information

Energy, whether input (as food) or output (as basal metabolism, digestion/absorption and physical activity), is measured in kilocalories. The kilocalorie (or Calorie with a capital *C*) is a measure of heat energy. The term *calorie* (small *c*) used in physics and chemistry is also a measure of heat energy. The difference is that it measures a smaller amount of heat energy, that is, it is 1/1000 of a kilocalorie or Calorie. One calorie is the amount of heat necessary to raise the temperature of one gram of water from 15 to 16° C. One thousand calories equal one kilocalorie or Calorie. Consequently, when we use the word *Calorie* (and we commonly do so) to refer to the energy bound in food or used through physical activity, we are really referring to *kilocalories*.

Materials Needed
butter or margarine (to represent fat: one-half stick)
corn starch (to represent carbohydrates: one-half cup)
unflavored dry gelatin powder placed in a nondescript container
    (to represent protein: one-half cup)
water (one-half cup)

Activity

vitamin pills (5 to 10: any vitamin or combination of them will suffice)
minerals (calcium pills, part of a bone or old teeth or anything that
   represents minerals; don't use iron because milk is a very poor source
   of iron)
six see-through containers (glasses are fine)
empty milk cartons (4 to 5; must be whole milk)
Energy Quiz

Part A

Put each of the first six materials listed above into a see-through
container and keep them out of sight. Place the empty milk carton on
the desk in the front of the room and challenge students with the
following questions:

1) What nutrients are found in whole milk? (*Fat, carbohydrate, protein,
   vitamins, minerals, and water.* As students correctly identify these
   substances, bring the containers into view.) Which nutrient has
   been taken out of skimmed milk? (*Fat*)
2) Which of the nutrients can provide us with energy? (*Fat,
   carbohydrate, and protein.* Single out these three on the
   containers.) Would you expect skimmed milk to supply as much
   energy as whole milk? (*Skimmed milk supplies much less energy
   than whole milk.* See the nutrition labels.)
3) What units do we use to measure the amount of energy in a food?
   In other words, when we talk about the amount of energy in a food,
   we usually say this food has a certain number of what? (*Calories.*
   For example, one eight-ounce glass of whole milk provides 160
   Calories.) (Pass the milk cartons around for the students to read
   the number of Calories and grams of fat, protein, and carbohydrate
   in whole milk. If you like, make an overnight assignment for
   students to find one food at home that gives this kind of
   information, and write down the brand name and related Calorie,
   protein, fat, and carbohydrate content per serving.)
4) What nutrients on this table do not supply us with energy?
   (*Vitamins, minerals, and water*)
5) If we didn't ingest vitamins, minerals, and water, would we be able
   to get the energy out of food (would we be able to get energy from
   fat, carbohydrate, and protein)? (*No.* Vitamins, minerals, and water
   help us get the energy out of food, that is, they help change food
   energy into energy our bodies can use in our cells.)

Part B

Students should complete the Energy Quiz.

Answer Key to Energy Quiz

Set A	Set C	Set D
1. food or fat cells	1. carbohydrates	1. yes
2. cells	proteins	2. yes
3. Calorie	fats	
4. fat cells	2. food energy	
Set B	3. vitamins	
1. Calories	minerals	
2. vitamins	water	
minerals		
water		

60

Questions on the Energy Quiz measure students' abilities to meet this lesson's objective. Thus, the quiz can be used as the evaluation for this lesson.

Pamphlets
"A Primer on Four Nutrients: Proteins, Carbohydrates, Fats, and Fiber." 1975. FDA Consumer, DHEW Publication No. (FDA) 75-2026, Government Printing Office, Superintendent of Documents, Washington, D.C. 20402. Free reprint. (T)
"Energy and Other Tricky Nutrition Words." 1978. United Fresh Fruit and Vegetable Association, 1019 Nineteenth Street., NW, Washington, D.C. 20036. Reprint. 50¢ (T)

Games
"The Calorie Game." 1972. Graphics Company, P.O. Box 331, Urbana, IL 61801. $9.95 (S)

Evaluation

References and Resources

Energy Quiz

Directions: Below are four sets of questions. Above each set of questions is a list of words. Read the questions. Then find the answer to each question in the word list and fill in the blanks.

Set A blood   food   Calorie
             cells   fat cells   stomach
             heat

_____ 1. Where does the energy your body uses come from?
_____ 2. Where does your body change the energy in food into the energy your body can use?
_____ 3. What do we call the unit we use to measure the amount of energy provided in food and the amount of energy required for activities?
_____ 4. Where does your body store any energy from food that it does not need?

Set B carbohydrates   proteins   water
             minerals   vitamins   Calories

_____ 1. Where you take the fat out of a food, what else do you lose?
_____ 2. What three nutrients do not give energy to your body?
_____
_____

Set C carbohydrates   lights   size
             fats   minerals   vitamins
             food energy   proteins   water

_____ 1. What three nutrients give energy to your body?
_____
_____
_____ 2. What do Calories measure?
_____ 3. What three nutrients help your body release energy from food?
_____
_____

Set D nutrients   no   yes
             maybe   no change   Calories

_____ 1. Do you burn any energy while you sleep?
_____ 2. Does your body use energy when you gaze at the stars?

Lesson 11
Calorie Input versus Output

Mathematics/Health/Art
Interdisciplinary Emphasis

The number of Calories you take into your body should equal but not be greater than the number your body needs for basal metabolism, digestion and absorption of food, and physical activity.
Concept

Given the Caloric values of food and the Caloric expenditure of various physical activities, students will
Objective

1) balance food inputs with energy outputs; and
2) identify Caloric input/output situations that illustrate positive and negative Caloric balance.

The main emphasis in this lesson is the relationship between energy put into the body and energy that leaves the body. This lesson will not delve into the technical aspects of how the potential energy in food is transformed in the cells into different kinds of energy the body needs to perform its functions. If you or your students wish to know more about energy production and transformation, please consult the textbooks listed in References and Resources.
Nutrition Information

Many of the questions posed in the activity deal with the concept of energy balance. Energy balance involves a complex set of occurrences. The body does not always achieve energy balance over a day's time. In fact, for humans the balancing of energy input and energy output often takes place over a week's time or more.

The amount of energy a person requires to accomplish a given task varies with that person's size, body composition, age, sex, state of health, the intensity of the activity being performed, and the duration of that activity. Because of all these variables, energy needs are individual needs. This is one reason activity charts such as the Energy Values of Activities chart, are not as precise as we would like to think. At best the Calories expressed in these charts are approximations of the amount of energy it would take for an individual to perform a given task. Determining the actual number of Calories burned during a specific activity requires more time and sophisticated measuring equipment than is usually available to the average person. Therefore, we rely on charts that tell us only roughly how much energy we are using.

Any excess energy taken into the body is usually stored as fat in fat

63

cells (adipose tissue) located all over the body. The body needs a certain amount of fat for good health. Today, though, few benefits result from having excess fat in the body. To reduce the amount of unnecessary fat, we have to "burn" or expend more energy than we take in. The problem arises in that getting rid of excess stored body fat is never as easy as the previous statement would have us believe. And for someone with the problem of being underweight, storing excess body fat may be just as difficult. Thus, if the topic of being overweight or underweight arises in your classroom, we offer the following advice:

• *Don't single out students for whom being underweight or being overweight is a problem* either to offer advice privately or to use as examples of the principles of energy balance for the class.

• If a child is underweight and *asks* how he or she might work to gain some additional weight, don't suggest either inactivity or consumption of high-energy, low-nutrient foods. Suggest instead moderate changes the child can make concerning the possible addition of food energy. Don't encourage eating and exercise patterns that may some day "backfire" on the child by contributing to a problem of overweight in his or her later years.

• If a child is overweight and *asks* how he or she might work to lose some excess body fat, don't immediately assume that the child is consuming excess food energy. Often the problem involves inactivity of the child. Encourage the child to decrease high-energy, low-nutrient foods *if overconsumption of these is a problem.* More importantly, though, encourage enjoyable physical exercise of all kinds to increase the child's energy expenditure. Research shows that activity need not be strenuous to affect body composition. Physical activity seems to benefit the body in cumulative ways. If a child is either extremely overweight or underweight, his or her problem *may* stem from a metabolic disorder. You should discuss the child's problem with the school nurse, who then may refer him or her to a physician or a registered dietitian in your area.

We emphasize a special caution concerning decreasing Calories in children. Children need nutrients *and* energy to grow properly. First, if the Calories are decreased, the child may find it more difficult to ingest the amounts and kinds of nutrients necessary for growth. Second, an adequate supply of energy is also very important to the growing body. Even if the amounts of other nutrients are adequate, if the energy supply is low, normal growth rate and possibly the health of the child will be affected.

Under the References and Resources section are listed some books students might enjoy reading about the special problems associated with being overweight. These problems very often apply to children who are also underweight. The stories can be used to develop class discussions on these topics if the children express an interest as they proceed through the assigned activities.

Trained health professionals in your school and your community can help if a child or a child's parents express concern with that child's amount of body fat. Although these professionals may be well equipped to handle weight maintenance problems, your role is important in the overall team effort. You are helping the child assume responsibility for managing his or her own weight.

Enclosed also in this lesson is a chart titled Energy Values of Foods. The energy-input values in this and all other such charts are approximate values, just as the energy-output values are. To be truly accurate, one would have to analyze a sample of all food prepared for each meal and each snack eaten. On the average, though, these charts provide energy-value figures that are adequate for day-to-day estimates.

Both the Energy Values of Activities and the Energy Values of Foods charts were adjusted so that the values noted are all multiples of fifteen. This modification in the values enables us to include "paper-clip equivalents" of all energy values given, thereby simplifying the students' tasks. One paper clip equals 15 Calories. Thus, we encourage you to use both charts as *estimates* of energy values and *not* as *exact measures* of energy input and output.

If you see a need to include foods not listed in the Energy Values of Foods chart, feel free to add them. In figuring the energy value of these new foods, remember to adjust the Calories to the nearest value that can be divided by fifteen and to include paper-clip equivalents.

One last word: it is not important that students remember exact energy values after completing these activities. What is important is that students have an idea of the relative energy value of various foods and the relative energy cost of various activities. It is also important that students can apply this knowledge to their own lives. The Energy We Use chart illustrates the relative energy cost of a few selected activities.

This activity will require 1½ to 2 hours of student time. It can be easily broken down into shorter time segments: Parts A and B; Part C; and Part D.

Activity

Materials Needed
a balance scale or materials to make your own simple balance:
    Model of Scale Balance
    a 20-centimeter strip of balsa wood or plastic straw
    a half-gallon milk carton, rinsed clean
    2 two-ounce paper cups (bathroom size)
    thread for suspending paper cups
    an 8-centimeter pin
paper clips: 3 boxes of 100 count
sand
5 ⁄ 8" index cards (about 60)
felt pens
bulletin board
pictures of foods and activities (optional)
paste (optional)
Energy We Use
Energy Values of Food
Energy Values of Activities
piece of clay
Understanding Energy, Parts I and II

You will need to Xerox one copy of Energy Values of Foods and Energy Values of Activities for use in Part B. Taking your Xeroxed copy of Energy Values of Foods, cut off and discard the right hand column "Number of Paper Clips." Then cut the remainder (horizontally) into 46 slips of paper. A sample slip would look like this:

apple	1 large	105 Cals.

Taking your Xeroxed copy of Energy Values of Activities, cut off and discard the two right-hand columns "Energy (Caloric) Output for TIme Given" and "Number of Paper Clips." Then cut the remainder (horizontally) into 25 slips of paper. An example slip could look like this:

badminton	5.25 Cals./min.	20 min.

Put both sets of slips into one container for students to draw from in Part B.

Prepare the simple balance as described below. You will be using it to demonstrate to students the concept of energy balance in Part C (question 8) of this activity. Also reproduce copies of the Energy Values of Activities chart for use at the end of Part C. Whether or not you give students individual copies of the other two charts (Energy We Use and Energy Values of Foods) is up to you. However, they are not to be given until the end of the activity.

Part A

Briefly, review with students the three major categories of energy expenditure: basal metabolism, digestion and absorption of food, and physical activity. Explain to them that the category they have the most control over is physical activity. Therefore, students who are more physically active will need more Calories than their less active peers. At this point, students should write down several (at least 7) physical activities and rank them according to which one burns the most Calories, the second most, down to the least. Students should save their lists for reevaluation after completion of this lesson.

Part B

Place the 71 thin strips of paper cut from the two charts into a container and instruct each student to draw two to three out (depending on the number of students in your class). At the same time, each student should be given a 3x5" index card for each slip of paper he or she has drawn. Then students should be given the following instructions:
1) For each slip of paper drawn listing an activity, the students must compute the "Energy Output for Activity Time" and the "Number of Paper Clips" this energy output would represent, remembering that one paper clip equals 15 Calories.
    a) Energy Output per Minute x Activity Time (minutes) = Energy Output for Activity Time
    b) Energy Output for Activity Time ÷ 15 Calories (one clip) = Number of Clips
2) For each slip of paper drawn listing a food, students must compute the "Number of Paper Clips" this energy input represents, remembering that one paper clip represents 15 Calories. (Energy Input ÷ 15 Calories (one clip) = Number of Clips)
3) For each slip of paper drawn, students should prepare an input *or* output 3x5" index card as follows:

Students can either draw pictures depicting the food or activity, or use magazine clippings and paste them on. When they are finished, students should sign their names on the backs and turn them in to you. At this point, you can check the cards for accuracy or spot check them as you

66

go through some of them in Part C. In any case, divide the cards into two decks (in preparation for Part C): Energy Input and Energy Output. Note: An alternative to steps 1 and 2 above would be to supply children with the answers needed to make the cards. Obviously time would be saved, but student involvement would be sacrificed.

Part C

Distribute the worksheet Understanding Energy, Part I, to the students. Explain that you will be using the cards they made to demonstrate the concept of energy balance. Your demonstration will follow the questions on the worksheet, which they should complete as you demonstrate.

Using the scale balance constructed earlier (or one you already had) and the deck of cards, guide students through the worksheet as follows:

Questions 1–3:
1) Turn over the top card on each of the two decks. Announce the name of the food and its "energy input." Announce the name of the activity and the length of time it took to complete the activity.
2) Take a class vote on whether or not this activity has a Caloric output less than, equal to, or greater than the Caloric input supplied by the food. Determine the correct answer by loading the balance scale with the correct number of paper clips: energy input into the left basket and energy output into the right basket. Announce the "Energy Output" value of the activity.
3) Repeat steps one and two at least five times or more (students need complete their worksheet for only three energy input-output situations.) Students should get progressively better at accurately estimating the energy output of an activity in relation to the energy input. For additional challenge, you may wish to discuss how much more or less time you would need to do an activity to bring input and output into equilibrium, that is, into perfect balance.

Questions 4–5:
1) Load the energy output side of the balance scale with the appropriate number of paper clips.
2) Go to the Input card deck, turn over a card, and announce the name and serving size of the food. Take a class vote on whether or not this amount of food would supply less than, about equal to, or more than

the number of Calories burned by the activity. Determine the correct answer by loading the energy input side of the scale with the correct number of paper clips. On the board, list the food, the amount, and its respective energy input. Repeat this process several times. Then discuss how the amounts of individual foods could be modified or combined to arrive at a figure quite close to the energy output of the activity. Students should fill in their answers with food(s) that would achieve approximate energy balance.

Questions 6–7:
   Basically, follow the same procedure as indicated for question 4 and 5. However, this time you are loading the energy input side of the scale first and looking at the energy output of various activities in terms of their relation to energy input.

Question 8:
   This can serve as a homework assignment if you desire. Hand out the chart Energy Values of Activities. You may wish to review the directions specified in the question with the students.

Answer Key to Understanding Energy, Part 1
1–3, 1–d. The answers to these questions depend on the cards drawn. The information students write down for part *a* of each question will be the basis for the answers in parts *b* through *d*.
4–7.   These answers also will vary depending on the cards drawn. In each case the total for the energy input or output values should approximate the energy value given in each problem.
8.   2,400 Calories. The energy output value for the activities listed should be equal to 2,400 Calories. Since it may be too difficult for students to balance the energy exactly, they may come up with answers that are slightly fewer or greater than 2,400 Calories.

Part D
   Distribute Part II of the worksheet Understanding Energy, dealing specifically with the relationship between energy input and output and body fat. To complete the worksheet, students have to refer to the chart Energy Values of Activities. Students should reevaluate their list of activities from Part A after they have completed the worksheet.

Answer Key to Understanding Energy, Part 2
   1. The pet would store the extra energy as fat.
   2. The body would store the extra energy as fat.
   3. You would lose weight because some body fat would have to be burned to supply the body with the extra energy it needs.
   4. Ride a bike.
   5. You burn more energy because your muscles work harder to lift you.
   6. Growth   repair
      maintenance   physical movement
   7. From fat cells.
   8. a. No change (adequate diet + adequate exercise = no change in body fat)
      b. Increase (adequate diet + inadequate exercise = increase in body fat)
      c. Decrease (adequate diet + more than adequate exercise = decrease in body fat)

9. a. Increase (excess Calories + inadequate exercise = increase in body fat)
  b. Increase (adequate diet + inadequate exercise = increased in body fat)
  c. No change (eating as many Calories as expended = no change in body fat)
  d. Decrease (eating fewer Calories than expended = decrease in body fat)
10. The answers to this question will vary. The activities listed, however, should be the ones that use at least 100 Calories per 30 minutes.

Questions 4 through 8 on Part I of the worksheet and questions 8 through 10 on Part II of the worksheet directly measure the students' ability to meet this lesson's objective. The following sample quiz could also be used.

__c__ 1. For dessert at dinner, John ate an extra piece of pecan pie. This gave him 400 more Calories than he burned up for the day. Which of the activities below would come nearest to burning up that extra food energy?
  a. badminton for 1 hour (energy output = 315 Calories)
  b. fishing for 2 hours (energy output = 300 Calories)
  c. ice skating for ¾ hour (energy output = 450 Calories)
  d. homework for 2½ hours (energy output = 260 Calories)
__d__ 2. Which of the situations below would result in a gain in body fat?
  a. Calorie input of 3,000 and Calorie output of 3,200
  b. Calorie input of 3,000 and Calorie output of 4,000
  c. Calorie input of 2,500 and Calorie output of 2,500
  d. Calorie input of 2,500 and Calorie output of 1,800
__b__ 3. Which of the situations below would result in a loss of body fat?
  a. Calorie input of 3,500 and Calorie output of 3,000
  b. Calorie input of 3,500 and Calorie output of 4,200
  c. Calorie input of 2,500 and Calorie output of 2,500
  d. Calorie input of 2,500 and Calorie output of 2,000

Books
Mayer, J. 1968. *Overweight: Causes, Cost, and Control.* Englewood Cliffs, N.J.: Prentice-Hall. $2.45 (T)
Nash, J. D., and Long, L. O. 1978. *Taking Charge of Your Weight and Well-Being.* Palo Alto: Bull Publishing Co. $9.95 (T)
Schneider, T. 1976. *Everybody's a Winner.* Boston: Little, Brown and Co. $4.94 (S)
Stuart, R. B., and Davis, B. 1972. *Slim Chance in a Fat World: Behavior Control of Obesity.* Champaign: Research Press. $6.95 (T)

Pamphlets
Konishi, F. 1973. "Exercise Equivalents of Food: A Practical Guide for Overweight." Carbondale, Ill.: Southern Illinois University Press. $1.95 (T)

Posters
"Calories: Food and Activity." No date (ca. 1975). Distribution Center, 7 Research Park, Cornell University, Ithaca, NY 14850. Nineteen Flipcharts. $1 (S,T)

Films/Filmstrips

Food, Energy, and You. 1978. Perennial Education, 477 Roger Williams, P.O. Box 855, Ravinia, Highland Park, IL 60035. Film, 16mm, color, sound, 11 minutes, study guide. $295/rental $29.50 (S)

Mulligan Stew: The Racer That Lost His Edge. 1972. Great Plains National Instructional Television Library, U.S. Dept. of Agriculture, Office of Communication Motion Picture Service, 14th and Independence, SW, Washington, D.C. 20250. $10 (S)

Articles

Jordan, H. P.; Kimbrell, G. M., and Levitz, L. S. 1976. "Managing Obesity: Why Diet Is Not Enough." *Postgraduate Medicine* 59:183–86 (April). (T)

Understanding Energy
(Part 1)

Today you are going to learn about energy. You'll see how the energy in food compares to the energy you "burn up" when you're active and when you're inactive. You'll even learn a little about balancing energy in your own body. Read the directions for this activity on the bulletin board. Then answer the questions below.

1. a. name of the food _____ name of activity _____
   energy input value _____ energy output value _____
   b. Does the scale balance? _____
   c. If not, which basket is heavier? _____
   d. Which basket do you suppose contains more energy? _____
2. a. name of the food _____ name of activity _____
   energy input value _____ energy output value _____
   b. Does the scale balance? _____
   c. If not, which basket is heavier _____
   d. Which basket do you suppose contains more energy? _____
3. a. name of the food _____ name of activity _____
   energy input value _____ energy output value _____
   b. Does the scale balance? _____
   c. If not, which basket is heavier? _____
   d. Which basket do you suppose contains more energy? _____
4. You went fishing for an hour and burned 150 Calories. What food or foods could you eat that would contain 150 Calories of energy?
   food(s) and amount   *energy input value*

   _____   _____

   _____   _____

5. You rode your bicycle with a friend for two full hours. That activity "burned" 600 Calories of energy. What food or foods could you eat that would contain that much energy?
   food(s) and amount   *energy input value*

   _____   _____

   _____   _____

6. You ate a strawberry shortcake. That strawberry shortcake contained 400 Calories. What activity or activities could you do to "burn up" that food energy?
   activity (and time)   *energy output value*

   _____   _____

   _____   _____

7. You ate an orange after school for a snack. The orange contained 75 Calories. What activity or activities could you do to "burn up" that food energy?
   activity (and time)   *energy output value*

   _____   _____

   _____   _____

8. If you ate a total of 2,400 Calories at meals and snacks today, how much energy would you need to "burn" to be in energy balance? _____ . Look at the activities on the Energy Values of Activities chart. Make a list of all the activities you could do today to burn energy. Write the "Activity Time" and energy output value of each activity beside it.

Name of Activity	Activity Time	Energy Output Value (Calories)
_____	_____	_____
_____	_____	_____
_____	_____	_____
_____	_____	_____
_____	_____	_____
_____	_____	_____
_____	_____	_____
_____	_____	_____
_____	_____	_____
_____	_____	_____
_____	_____	_____
_____	_____	_____
_____	_____	_____
_____	_____	_____
_____	_____	_____
_____	_____	_____

Now add all the Energy Output Values. Do you come up with a number less than, equal to, or greater than 2,400 Calories? If your sum is greater than 2,400 Calories, circle those activities you would do that would make your sum about equal to 2,400 Calories. If your sum is less than 2,400 Calories, add more activities to bring your sum up to about 2,400 Calories.

Don't forget, when your energy input is equal to your energy output, we say you are in "energy balance."

Understanding Energy
(Part 2)

1. What would happen if you had a pet and your pet ate more energy than he or she "burned up"? _____
_____

2. What would happen to your body if you ate more energy than you burned up? ___
_____

3. What would happen to your body if your body "burned" more energy than you ate? _____
_____

4. Will you burn more energy if you sit or if you ride a bike? _____
_____

5. Why do you suppose you would burn more energy when you climb stairs than when you walk on level ground? _____
_____

6. What's happening to your body when you are sleeping that makes it need energy? _____
_____

7. Your body needs nutrients and energy. Today you ate all the nutrients your body needs to be healthy. You were really active. You played ball, ran, bicycled, and helped your mom clean the attic. Your body needs a little more energy, but there is no food around. Where will your body get the extra energy it needs? _____
_____

8. You can't take off your skin and look in a mirror to see exactly how much body fat you have. You can imagine how much there is, though. When you look in the mirror, you can imagine whether your body fat is decreasing, increasing, or staying the same. How do you think these children imagine their body fat? (If your answer is *no change* in body fat, write N.C. in the blank under the last picture in the row. If your answer is an *increase* in body fat, draw this arrow ↑ in the blank. If your answer is *decrease* in body fat, draw this arrow ↓ in the blank.)

A.

2,400 INPUT   2,400 OUTPUT   _____ IN BODY FAT

B. 2,400 INPUT   1,500 OUTPUT   _____ IN BODY FAT

C. 2,400 INPUT   3,000 OUTPUT   _____ IN BODY FAT

9. Fill in the blanks at the end of each row with the correct answer, just as you did in Question B.

A. 3,000 INPUT   2,000 OUTPUT   _____ IN BODY FAT

B. 2,400 INPUT   2,000 OUTPUT   _____ IN BODY FAT

2,000 INPUT   2,000 OUTPUT   _____ IN BODY FAT

1,500 INPUT   2,000 OUTPUT   _____ IN BODY FAT

10. You just went to the doctor with your dad for a checkup. In her office the doctor measured your body in a special way that told her how much fat your body contains. She told you that your body is made of many things, and fat is one of them. She also told you that your body needs some of that fat. Why? The answer is that you need body fat for the following purposes:

● to insulate you from the heat and cold

● to pad some of your organs and act as a shock absorber for your body and organs

● to provide you with extra energy when you can't get that energy from food

She asked you to look in the full-length mirror and tell her how you saw your body. Do you have too much body fat, too little, or just the right amount? You told her you thought you might have too much. She agreed. Your body has more fat than it really needs.

After asking you and your dad about the foods you eat, she thought a minute. She decided that since you are eating a healthful diet, you should *not* cut out any nutrients or food energy. But she suggested that you try to think of fun ways to "burn" some extra energy.

Make a list of ten activities you would like to do alone or with a friend to help your body "burn up" extra energy. (You may include activities from the activity card deck Energy Values of Activities chart or think of some of your own.)

Ten activities to "burn up" extra energy:

Energy output values:

_____   _____
_____   _____
_____   _____
_____   _____
_____   _____
_____   _____
_____   _____
_____   _____
_____   _____
_____   _____

ENERGY WE USE

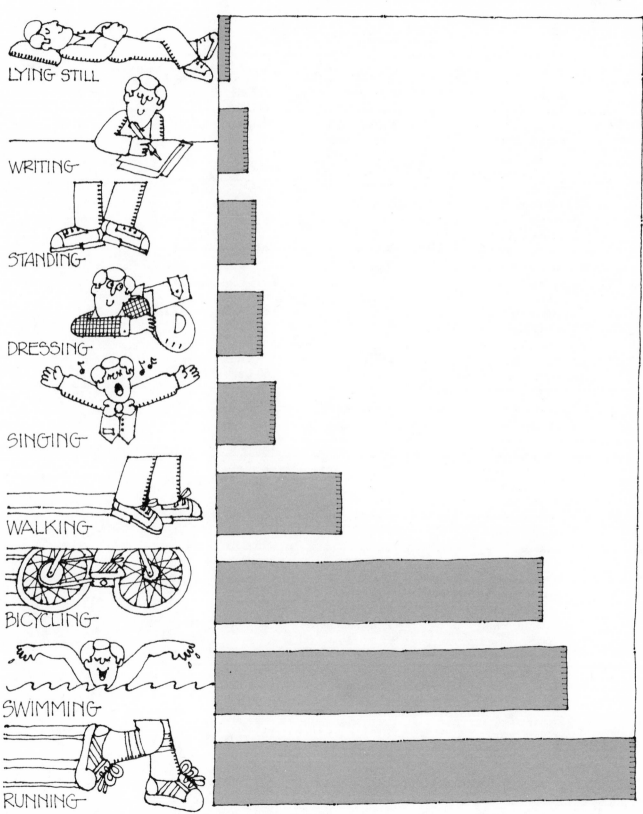

LYING STILL

WRITING

STANDING

DRESSING

SINGING

WALKING

BICYCLING

SWIMMING

RUNNING

Energy Values of Foods

Food	Size or Measure	Energy (Caloric) Input	Number of Paper Clips 1 clip = 15 calories
apple	1 large	105 Cals.	7
bacon	2 strips	90 Cals.	6
banana	1 small	90 Cals.	6
bread and butter	1 pat, 1 slice	90 Cals.	6
cake	1/10 of cake	345 Cals.	23
carbonated beverages	240 ml.	105 Cals.	7
candy, hard	30 g.	105 Cals.	7
caramel	30 g.	120 Cals.	7
carrot	90 g.	45 Cals.	3
cereal with milk & sugar	30 g.	210 Cals.	14
cheddar cheese	30 g.	120 Cals.	7
chicken, fried	½ breast	225 Cals.	15
chocolate candy bar	42 g.	210 Cals.	14
chocolate-chip cookie	1 cookie	60 Cals.	4
chocolate fudge	30 g.	120 Cals.	7
doughnut	1	150 Cals.	10
egg, fried	1	105 Cals.	7
egg, boiled	1	75 Cals.	5
hamburger and bun	1	360 Cals.	24
hamburger, french fries, and coke	1 serving each	750 Cals.	50
ice cream	90 g.	195 Cals.	13
ice cream soda	1	255 Cals.	17
ice milk	90 g.	150 Cals.	10
jello with cream	80 g.	120 Cals.	7
jelly beans	9 beans	60 Cals.	4
milk shake	240 ml.	420 Cals.	28
milk, whole	240 ml.	165 Cals.	11
milk, skimmed	240 ml.	90 Cals.	6
orange	1	75 Cals.	5
orange juice	240 ml.	120 Cals.	8
pancake with syrup	1	120 Cals.	8
peach, raw	1 medium	45 Cals.	3
peach, canned in heavy syrup	2 medium halves	75 Cals.	5
peach, canned in own juice	2 medium halves	45 Cals.	3
pie, apple	⅛ pie	285 Cals.	19
pizza	⅛ pie	180 Cals.	12
pork chop	1	315 Cals.	21
potato chips	10 chips	105 Cals.	7
potato, french fries	10	137 Cals.	9
spaghetti with meat sauce	250 g.	330 Cals.	22
steak	90 g.	225 Cals.	15
strawberry shortcake	1	405 Cals.	27
yogurt, plain	1 cup	120 Cals.	8
yogurt, flavored	1 cup	240 Cals.	16

Energy Values of Activities

Activity	Energy (Caloric) Output per Minute	Activity Time	Energy (Caloric) Output For Activity Time	No. of Paper Clips 1 clip = 15 Calories
Badminton	5.25 Cals./Min.	20 min.	105	7
Baseball	6.0 Cals./Min.	1 hour	120	8
Bicycling	5.0 Cals./Min	1 hour	300	20
Classroom work	2.2 Cals./Min.	5 hours	660	44
Climbing stairs or hills	20.0 Cals./Min.	15 min	300	20
Dancing fast	9.75 Cals./Min.	20 min.	195	13
Dodgeball	9.75 Cals./Min.	20 min.	195	13
Eating a meal	1.5 Cals./Min.	20 min.	30	2
Eating a snack	1.5 Cals./Min.	10 min.	15	1
Fishing	2.5 Cals./Min.	1 hour	150	10
Frisbee	4.5 Cals./Min.	20 min.	90	6
Homework	1.75 Cals./Min.	1 hour	105	7
Household chores	3.0 Cals./Min.	1 hour	180	12
Ice skating	10.0 Cals./Min.	1 hour	600	40
Practicing musical instrument	2.5 Cals./Min.	1 hour	150	10
Reading	1.5 Cals./Min.	30 min.	45	3
Running	19.5 Cals./Min.	20 min.	390	26
Skateboard	4.5 Cals./Min.	20 min.	90	6
Sleeping	1.0 Cals./Min.	8 hours	480	32
Swimming	13.5 Cals./Min.	30 min.	405	27
Tag	9.75 Cals./Min.	20 min.	195	13
Touch football	8.25 Cals./Min.	20 min.	165	11
Volleyball	7.5 Cals./Min.	20 min.	150	10
Walking	5.2 Cals./Min.	1 hour	315	21
Washing and dressing	3.3 Cals./Min.	1 hour	195	13
Watching television	1.5 Cals./Min.	1 hour	90	6

Lesson 12
Fats in Foods

Health

Fats provide more than twice as much energy as protein or carbohydrate.
  Foods high in fat are high in Calories.

After completing a worksheet acquainting students with the amount of fat in various foods, students should be able to differentiate between high-fat and low-fat foods with 80 percent accuracy.

Overweight people are often described as fat. This description is accurate for many people because any excess food energy from any source is stored in the body as fat. Ounce for ounce, fats supply more than twice as much energy as either carbohydrate or protein. One can gain weight very rapidly if a lot of fats are eaten and the total Caloric intake exceeds Caloric needs.
  However, body fat is not limited to overweight persons. Everybody has some fat stored in their body. These stores supply energy and also act as cushions for the body and its organs. For example, layers of fatty tissue in the palms of the hands, the soles of the feet, and the buttocks serve as firm pads against exterior pressure. Surrounding the eyes are protective fatty cushions. Deposits of fat under the skin also act as insulators that prevent rapid loss of heat. Fat is also needed to carry the fat soluble vitamins A, D, E, and K.
  Biochemists discovered that diets containing no fat were nutritionally deficient and caused scaly skin, slow growth, and lowered resistance to infection. They concluded that a certain *fatty acid** cannot be made by the human body and therefore must be provided by the diet. This essential fatty acid is linoleic acid. The requirement for this fatty acid is small, approximately 2 percent of the daily Caloric intake. Abundant amounts of linoleic acid are found in vegetable oils.

Materials Needed
Fats in Foods (Appendix G)

Interdisciplinary Emphasis

Concepts

Objective

Nutrition Information

Activity

---
*The building blocks of fat are fatty acids attached to glycerol, which is a simple alcohol. When three fatty acids are combined with glycerol, the fat is called a triglyceride.

High-E or Low-E
The Basic Four Food Groups (Appendix B)

Have the students complete the worksheet High-E or Low-E and discuss the following questions in class.
1) Did you have trouble placing some foods in a food group?
   (Yes. The basic four food groups do not include all the foods that are eaten, particularly fats, oils, and sweets. Specific examples are mayonnaise, potato chips, corn oil, and chocolate candy. Foods that do not fit into one of the basic four food groups are called additional, miscellaneous, or other foods.)
2) What food groups contain a lot of fat?
   (meat group, milk group, and some foods found in the additional foods.)
   What food groups contain small amounts of fat?
   (items in the fruit and vegetable group and the breads and cereal group contain small amounts of fat. Skimmed milk is one food item in the milk group low in fat.)
3) Whole milk contains more calories per glass than skimmed milk. Can you use the table to prove it?
   (A glass of whole milk contains 9.0 grams of fat, while a glass of skimmed milk contains only 0.2 grams of fat. Therefore, whole milk has more Calories per glass than skimmed milk because it contains more fat.)
4) Are the foods *lower* in fat most likely to be from animal or plant sources?
   (plant sources)

Answer Key to High-E or Low-E

High E rank	food and amount	total fat in grams	source	food group
1 highest	hamburger: ¼ lb.	23.0	animal	meat
2 highest	hot dog: 1	16.0	animal	meat
3 third highest	corn oil	14.0	plant	⎧ these foods
4 fourth highest	mayonnaise: 1 T	11.2	plant and animal	not in any of the four food groups
5 fifth highest	potato chips: 12	11.0	plant	
6 sixth highest	cheese: 1 ounce	9.1	animal	milk
7 seventh highest	whole milk: 1 cup	9.0	animal	milk
8 eighth highest	choc. bar: 1¾ oz	8.9	plant	⎧ not in any of the four food groups
9 ninth highest	butter: 2 pats	8.2	plant	meat
10 tenth highest	bacon: 2 slices	8.1	animal	meat

Low E rank	food	total fat in grams	source	food group
1 lowest	rice	.1	plant	bread and cereal
2 second lowest	broccoli	.2	plant	fruit and veg.
3 third lowest	skim milk	.3	animal	milk

82

4 fourth lowest	orange	.5	plant	fruit and veg.
5 fifth lowest	corn	.6	plant	fruit and veg.
6 sixth lowest	whole wheat bread	.9	plant	bread and cereal

__L__ 1. 1 apple
__H__ 2. 10 french fries
__L__ 3. 1 baked potato, plain
__L__ 4. glass of skimmed milk
__H__ 5. cheeseburger with mayonnaise and pickles
__H__ 6. peanut-butter sandwich
__H__ 7. hot dog wrapped in bacon and cheese
__(1 tsp. of butter)__ 8. Would you get more energy from spreading a slice of bread with 1 tsp. of butter or 1 tsp. of jelly?
__(They are listed as fats)__ 9. Shortening, butter, margarine, and vegetable cooking oil have something in common. What is it?

Books

Collipp, P. J. 1975. *Childhood Obesity*. Acton, Mass.: Publishing Sciences Group. $9.50 (T)

Gilbert, S. 1975. *Fat Free: Commonsense for Young Weight Worriers*. New York: MacMillan Publishing Co. $5.95 (S,T)

Lipsyte, R. 1977. *One Fat Summer*. New York: Harper and Row. $1.75 (S)

Perly, L. 1976. *Me and Fat Glenda*. New York: Pocket Books. $1.25 (S)

Pamphlets

"Food Fat." 1978. United Fresh Fruit and Vegetable Association, 1019 Nineteenth Street, NW, Washington, D.C. 20036. 50¢ (T)

Booklets

Deutsch, R. M. 1978. "The Fat Counter Guide." Palo Alto: Bull Publishing Company. $1.95 (T)

Eden, A. N., and Heilman, J. R. 1975. "Growing Up Thin." New York: Berkeley Publishing Corp. $1.50 (T)

Articles

"The Nature of Weight Loss During Short-Term Dieting." 1978. *Nutrition Reviews* 36: 72–74 (March). (T)

High-E or Low-E Foods

Directions: You have been given a food composition table labeled Fats in Food. Study the list of foods and their total fat content. List in order the ten foods having the largest amount of fat in them.

rank	food and amount	total fat in grams	source (animal or plant)	food group
highest	_____	_____	_____	_____
second highest	_____	_____	_____	_____
third highest	_____	_____	_____	_____
fourth highest	_____	_____	_____	_____
fifth highest	_____	_____	_____	_____
sixth highest	_____	_____	_____	_____
seventh highest	_____	_____	_____	_____
eighth highest	_____	_____	_____	_____
ninth highest	_____	_____	_____	_____
tenth highest	_____	_____	_____	_____

Now list the six foods having the least amount of fat.

rank	food and amount	total fat in grams	source (animal or plant)	food group
lowest	_____	_____	_____	_____
second lowest	_____	_____	_____	_____
third lowest	_____	_____	_____	_____
fourth lowest	_____	_____	_____	_____
fifth lowest	_____	_____	_____	_____
sixth lowest	_____	_____	_____	_____

Use this table to answer some discussion questions raised by your teacher.

Lesson 13
Find the Fat

Mathematics

Interdisciplinary Emphasis

Animal foods tend to contain more fat than plant foods. We cannot always see the fat in a food. Hot dogs, cheese, and nuts are good examples of foods containing "hidden fat."

Concepts

Given two or more meals, students should be able to identify the meal lower in fat.

Objective

Foods that are high in fat are also high in Calories. Many times these foods can be easily identified, such as vegetable oil, butter, margarine, bacon, and sausage. Unfortunately all high-fat foods do not display their fat content as readily as those foods already mentioned. Examples of foods containing hidden fat are cakes, cookies, nuts, peanut butter, and meat. Lean beef and pork can be very high in fat because of the marbling. The method of food preparation can also increase the amount of hidden fat. Foods that are fried will usually contain more fat than broiled foods, from which the fat is allowed to drain off.

Nutrition Information

Materials Needed
white onion skin or brown grocery paper
Fats in Foods (Appendix G)
food samples (choose at least 6)

Activity

shortening	meat scraps
margarine	chocolate
apple	peanut butter
pie crust	mayonnaise
cooking oil	minced coconut
sugar	drop of whole milk
saltine cracker	drop of skimmed milk
cookie	bread
hot dog	

Part A
   Write the food samples on the board and ask the students to write on a piece of paper the foods that are high in fat. Rub a sample of food from the list on a piece of white onion skin or brown grocery paper. Let

them dry and then hold the paper up to the light. If a greasy spot remains on the paper, fat is present. (You may wish to assign a sample to each student and have them report their results to the class.) Go on to Part B while the onion skin or grocery paper is drying.

Part B

This exercise should improve the students' ability to recognize foods high in fat. Ask them this question: "If your mother was watching her weight, which lunch do you think she would select?"

Lunch 1	*Lunch 2*
¼ lb. hamburger, no bun	cheese sandwich: 1 oz. American
½ cup peas with 2 pats butter	cheese on 2 slices whole-
1 glass whole milk (8 oz.)	wheat bread
½ fresh tomato	1 glass skimmed milk (8 oz.)
	1 medium apple

Have the students calculate the number of grams of fat in each lunch using the food composition table, Fats in Foods. Lunch 1 has 40.2 grams of fat while Lunch 2 has 11.1 grams of fat.

Time allowing, you may want to examine one or more school lunch menus for their fat content. You could also have students analyze meals at home.

Evaluation

Part B requires an accurate calculation of the total grams of fat in each lunch menu. Students should select Lunch 1 as having more Calories from fat than Lunch 2 and show calculations.

References and Resources

Pamphlets

"Calorie Controlled Meatless Meals." No date. Loma Linda Foods, General Offices, 11503 Pierce Street, Riverside, CA 92515. Free. (T)

"The Ungreasy Spoon." 1978. Center for Science in the Public Interest, P.O. Box 7226, Washington, DC 20044. $1.50/10 (T)

Booklets

"Questions and Answers about Fats and Oils in Our Foods." No date. Best Foods, Nutrition Information Service, Box 307, Coventry, CT 06238. First copy free/bulk rates available. (T)

Films/Filmstrips

Low-Fat Meat Preparation. 1975. International Producers Services, 351 Twanda West, Hollywood, CA 90068. Film, 16mm, color, sound, 14 minutes $250 (S,T)

Lesson 14
Simple versus Complex

Language Arts

The carbohydrates are a class of nutrients containing sugars (simple carbohydrate) and fiber and starch (complex carbohydrate).

After completing the worksheets, each student should be able to identify food sources of complex carbohydrates and explain why they are preferred nutritionally over high-sugar foods.

Carbohydrates are a class of nutrients that provide energy. Our bodies are able to obtain energy also from protein and fat. Foods high in carbohydrate include legumes, bread, cereals, vegetables, and fruits. The American diet derives 40 to 50 percent of its Calories from carbohydrates. Some populations in the world derive up to 80 percent of their total Caloric intake from carbohydrates. It is the most readily available and digestible form of fuel for energy. In the United States significant changes in the carbohydrate ingestion pattern have occurred. More and more of the carbohydrates in the American diet are coming from simple carbohydrates. Simple carbohydrates are sugars. All simple carbohydrates have a varying degree of sweetness. Fructose and sucrose (table sugar) have a high sweetening power. Other simple carbohydrates include glucose, lactose, galactose, and maltose. Complex carbohydrates are composed of hundreds or thousands of glucose molecules linked together in various ways. Fiber is a type of complex carbohydrate. It is not digested by the human digestive tract because humans do not have the enzymes capable of breaking the chemical bonds. Starch is a complex carbohydrate that is digestible. Foods high in starch include legumes, breads, cereals, and some vegetables.

Complex carbohydrates are the preferred dietary carbohydrate for several reasons. Foods high in complex carbohydrate usually provide other essential nutrients as well as energy in the form of starch. Legumes are a good source of protein as well as carbohydrate. Vegetables provide several vitamins and minerals in addition to starch. Foods high in starch that have not been refined contribute fiber, which provides certain health benefits. High-sugar foods frequently do not provide any other nutrients in significant amounts. Consumption of sugar-dense foods are negative factors cited in oral health care. In later lessons the relationship of simple

Interdisciplinary Emphasis

Concept

Objective

Nutrition Information

carbohydrate to dental caries will be examined in more detail.

The Senate Select Committee on Nutrition and Human Needs was formed in 1966 in response to the widespread discovery of nutrition-related conditions in all parts of the United States. Inadequate nutrition and diet-related diseases, such as obesity and heart disease, were found to occur in large numbers. The formation of this committee was the first step toward forming a national nutrition policy. The Senate Select Committee recognized the strong relationship of diet to our environment and set up practical guides or "dietary goals" for the United States as a whole. These goals deal with changes in food selection and preparation. The second edition of the dietary goals proposed by the Senate Select Committee are included in this lesson.

Carbohydrates are popularly associated with quick energy. Students should see that not all carbohydrates provide the same nutritional contributions. This lesson encourages students to be discriminating in their choices of desserts and snacks, conforming to the new dietary goals presented by the Senate Select Committee on Nutrition.*

Dietary Goals for the United States
Second Edition
1. To avoid overweight, consume only as much energy (number of Calories) as is expended: if overweight, decrease energy intake and increase energy expenditure.
2. Increase the consumption of complex carbohydrates and naturally occurring sugars from about 28 percent of energy intake to about 48 percent of energy intake.
3. Reduce the consumption of refined and processed sugars by about 45 percent to account for about 10 percent of total energy intake.
4. Reduce fat consumption from 40 percent to 30 percent of energy intake.
5. Reduced saturated fat consumption to account for about 10 percent of total energy intake; and balance that with polyunsaturated and mono-unsaturated fats, which account for about 10 percent of energy intake each.
6. Reduce cholesterol consumption to about 300 milligrams a day.
7. Limit the intake of sodium by reducing the intake of salt to about 5 grams a day.

Activity

Note: Several days before this lesson is to be taught, ask your students to save cereal boxes to be brought to class. If possible, one serving should be left in the box. You may wish to collect a supply for use by those students who neglect to bring their own cereal boxes. A couple of these boxes should be saved for use in lesson 16 as well.

Materials Needed
A Good Lick
Flour Power
blackboard
clock with a second hand
paper cups
water for drinking
small food samples for tasting (see suggested foods in Part B)

---

*The full report of the Dietary Goals for the U.S. is available from the Government Printing Office, Washington, DC 20402. Stock Number 070-04376-8. $2.30.

Part A

Have the students read and complete the worksheet Flour Power. You may want to go over the answers to the worksheet in class before proceeding to Part B of the activity.

Answer Key to Flour Power

1. any plant food (grains, cereals, nuts, legumes, vegetables, or fruits)
2. Simple carbohydrate, complex carbohydrate
3. fiber
4. protein, vitamins, and minerals
5. sucrose
6. no
7. candy, gum, soft drinks, fudge, cake with icing, sherbet, and others
8. The reason is that sugar left in contact with the teeth leads to acid production and subsequent tooth decay. Students *are not* given this information in Flour Power and thus their answers will be postulates. Refer back to this question after completing the next two lessons.
9. First Choice: whole grains and cereals
   Second Choice: refined flour, fresh fruits, and vegetables
   Last Choice: foods high in sucrose
10. Answers will vary, but should convey the idea that foods high in complex carbohydrate and low in sugar are nutritionally desirable because they a) usually provide protein, vitamins, and minerals, and b) do not promote tooth decay.

Part B

In this part of the activity students will, by sight and taste, estimate relative amounts of sweetness in foods containing carbohydrate. Foods containing sugar will taste sweet immediately. Students may even be able to distinguish relative intensities of sweetness. When applicable, food labels should be checked against lists of ingredients on labels. Since artificial sweeteners are used by some companies, this test is valid only for those foods that are known to use sugar as the only sweetener. Since there are different kinds of sugars, any of these will qualify: table sugar, sucrose, dextrose, levulose, fructose, corn syrup, corn sweeteners, or honey.

Distribute to students copies of A Good Lick. Divide students into pairs, with each pair assigned to one of the carbohydrate food groups. Instruct students to read carefully the directions found on the worksheet A Good Lick. Demonstrate steps 3 through 6 for one food before the students perform on their own. Point out the necessity of waiting and noting the appearance of sweet taste.

Suggested foods to be tried might include:

dry cereals group
unsweetened dry cereals
presweetened cereals
uncooked hot cereal mixes

breads
whole grain breads
enriched white breads
sandwich bread, hot dog roll, or
    hamburger roll

raw vegetable group

celery	turnip
carrot	green pepper
lettuce	peas

cracker group
saltines
graham crackers
party crackers

fruit group		pastries and sweets group	
apple	banana	cake or cupcake	
orange or grapefruit		doughnut	candy
fresh peach or pear		breakfast roll	
grapes		cookies	

Place on the blackboard the following grid.

A Good Lick Class Record

Dry-Cereal Foods	High Sugar	Low Sugar	?	Pastry and Sweet Foods	High Sugar	Low Sugar	?
1				1			
2				2			
3				3			
Bread Foods				Fruit Foods			
1				1			
2				2			
3				3			
Cracker Foods				Vegetable Foods			
1				1			
2				2			
3				3			

For each food listed ask the student if he or she thinks it is high in sugar or low in sugar. When all foods have been recorded, ask students which groups of food are mostly complex carbohydrate and which are simple carbohydrate. Fruit foods may be ranked as ??. These foods contain both simple and complex carbohydrates, which may cause some confusion for students assigned this food group. If students are not sure of other foods, have them check the food labels.

Answer Key to A Good Lick
1. By experience, you may recognize pastries or candies as having sugar. Except for powdered or granular sugar, the presence of sugar is difficult to see.
2. ingredients list on the label, tasting
3. complex carbohydrates found in foods made of whole grain flour
4. foods containing high amounts of refined sugar (sucrose, corn syrup, etc.)
5. will vary, but should follow ranking found in Flour Power
6. will vary

Have students return to the worksheet A Good Lick to complete the answer for number 6.

Evaluation   The evaluation of the lesson may be accomplished by checking the conclusions following the analysis of data from the class. The conclusions should indicate that energy foods are most desirable if they have a relatively high amount of complex carbohydrates (flour) and a small amount of refined sugar. A second conclusion should include the explanation that sugar causes dental caries. The following test items may also be administered.

__c__ 1. Your class tested six different groups of food. From which group should you select your snack?
   a. pastries
   b. candies
   c. fruit
   d. cookies

__a__ 2. Sometimes you feel a need for something sweet. Which food is sweet, but contains low amounts of table sugar?
   a. grapes
   b. doughnut
   c. chocolate cake
   d. hard candy

__b__ 3. Some young persons like to munch on cereal while they watch television. Which snack would be the best choice?
   a. presweetened cereal
   b. unsweetened cereal
   c. unsweetened cereal with sugar
   d. no starchy food is good

__c__ 4. In which food will you expect to find complex carbohydrates?
   a. eggs
   b. meat
   c. potatoes
   d. yogurt

__d__ 5. Some persons give up macaroni so they can eat candy snacks for energy. Is this a good way to think about dieting?
   a. No. All carbohydrates are bad for you because they cause tooth decay.
   b. Yes, because candy has fewer calories than macaroni.
   c. Yes, because starchy foods are fattening.
   d. No, because complex carbohydrates are a better food value.

Books
Mayer, C. 1971. *The Bread Book*. New York: Harcourt Brace Jovanovich. $6.95. (S)

Pamphlets
"Fred: The Horse Who Likes Bread." 1975. U.S. Department of Agriculture, Office of Communication, Room 207A, 14th and Independence, SW, Washington, DC 20250. Activity leaflet. Free. (S)
"Questions Most Frequently Asked about Sugar." 1975. The Sugar Association, 254 West 31st Street, New York, NY 10001. Free. (T)
"Sugars in Nutrition." 1977. United Fresh Fruit and Vegetable Association, 1019 Nineteenth Street, NW, Washington, DC 20036. Reprint. 65.. (T)

Posters
"Eat Whole Grains." 1975. Center for Science in the Public Interest, 1757 S St., NW, Washington, DC 20009. $2 (S)
"Grains in Your World." 1976. Quaker Oaks Company, Merchandise Mart Plaza, Chicago, IL 60654. Eight spirit masters. Free. (S)

References
and
Resources

Films/Filmstrips

Earthbread. 1973. Bullfrog Films, Box 114, Milford Square, PA 18935. Film, 16mm, color, sound, 20 minutes. $250/$25 rental. (S)

Wandering Waldo, Wheat Nutrition Through the Ages. 1976. Evans/ Pacific, Seattle, WA 20005. Film, 16mm, color, sound, 18 minutes. Free rental. (S)

Articles

Greenberg, F. 1977. "An Introduction to Grains." *Redbook Magazine* pp. 116–75 (October). (T)

Hardy, S. L.; Brennarn, C. P.; and Wyse, B. W. 1979. "Fructose: Comparison with Sucrose As Sweetener in Four Products." *Journal of the American Dietetic Association* 74:41–46 (January). (T)

Flour Power

In the last lesson we saw that fat was hidden in some foods. Today we will try foods that give us carbohydrates, a class of nutrients that give our bodies energy. Some carbohydrates have better food value than others.

There are two kinds of carbohydrates: complex and simple. Starch is a complex carbohydrate. It is found in plant foods. 1. Can you name some foods that contain complex carbohydrates? _____

Grains and cereals are good sources of complex carbohydrates. These foods also have protein, vitamins, and minerals. Flour, used to make bread, comes from grain. Other sources of complex carbohydrates include fruits and vegetables.

You may recall that foods (in their natural state) high in starch are enclosed by fiber. Examples of such foods include potatoes, kidney and lima beans, sunflower seeds, and whole wheat flour. Whole wheat flour contains the fiber from the grain that gives the flour the brown color. Fiber is a complex carbohydrate that our bodies cannot digest. It takes longer for our bodies to get the energy from complex carbohydrate than from simple carbohydrate. 2. Name the two types of carbohydrates in food. _____ and _____. 3. What complex carbohydrate can't we digest? _____ 4. Foods high in complex carbohydrates usually have other nutrients besides starch. What other nutrients do these foods have? _____

The second type of carbohydrate is called simple carbohydrate. Simple carbohydrates are sugars. Table sugar is one example. It is called *sucrose* by biochemists. Corn syrup, corn sweeteners, and invert sugars are mixtures of glucose and fructose. We refer to table sugar, brown sugar, corn syrups and sweeteners, and invert sugar as "refined and processed" sugars. Simple carbohydrates are absorbed by the body faster than complex carbohydrates. Foods high in refined and processed sugars often contain other nutrients in very small amounts or not at all. Examples of foods high in refined and processed sugars are pancake syrup, jam, jelly, sherbet, candy, fudge, gum, soda, and cakes with icing. Therefore, complex carbohydrates are a better value than foods high in sugar.

In the next few lessons we will see how high-sugar foods can affect our dental health. Sugar left in contact with the teeth helps to develop tooth decay.

The U.S. Dietary Goals are guidelines that have been proposed for all Americans. They suggest that we should try to use carbohydrates in our diets in this order:

First Choice: whole grains and cereals (complex carbohydrates with high fiber content)

Second Choice: refined flour (complex carbohydrates with low fiber content) fresh fruits and vegetables

Last Choice: foods high in refined and processed sugars (simple carbohydrates)

In the next part of this activity we will test some foods for the type of carbohydrate in them. 5. What do biochemists call table sugar? _____ 6. Do foods that are full of refined and processed sugars usually provide us with other nutrients? _____ 7. Name three examples of foods high in these types of sugar. _____ , _____ , and _____ .

8. High-sugar foods promote tooth decay. How might this happen?

_____

_____

9. What do the Dietary Goals recommend when one is choosing carbohydrate foods?

_____

_____

_____

_____

10. Why is this worksheet called "Flour Power?"

_____

_____

_____

_____

A Good Lick

The experiment should be done this way. You and a partner will be assigned to test one of these groups of foods: dry-cereal foods, bread foods, cracker foods, pastry and sweet foods, vegetable foods, and fruit foods. You should test separately, three foods from your assigned group. Here are the steps.

Step 1. Select a partner and decide who will be the taster and who will be the timer.

Step 2. The timer should get equal sized portions of the foods to be tested. The taster should get a paper cup of water.

Step 3. The taster should begin chewing a sample of food when the timer says, "Begin." The timer will count the number of seconds by using a watch or a clock with a sweep second hand.

Step 4. The taster should hold up his hand when sweetness is first tasted.

Step 5. The timer will write on the data sheet the number of seconds it took the taster to taste sweetness. Do not record after 60 seconds.

Step 6. The taster should drink some water before selecting a new sample of food. Begin with step 3 again.

After all food samples are tested, complete questions 1 through 5 at the end of this worksheet. Then report your results of the food testing to your teacher, who will record them on the blackboard.

Good Lick Data Record

Food Name	Seconds	How would you rate the food?		
		Very Sweet	Not Too Sweet	Not Sweet
1.				
2.				
3.				

Answer these questions:

1. By looking at the foods, can you tell which ones contain lots of sugar? _____

2. In what two ways can you determine the presence of sugar in any food? _____

3. U.S. Dietary Goals suggest which type of carbohydrate as the first choice? _____

4. Which carbohydrate is the last choice? _____

5. Look at your data record to see which foods are low in sugar. Of the foods you tested, which is best for you? _____

After you have given your results to your teacher, wait until he or she directs you to complete #6 of this worksheet.

6. After you have looked at the data from the whole class, write a conclusion. It should state which kinds of foods have the highest amount of complex carbohydrates while having the least amount of simple sugars. Write what evidence permits you to make that conclusion.

Lesson 15
Boxes and Cubes

Mathematics	Interdisciplinary Emphasis

The amount of table sugar (sucrose) in equal amounts of two different foods may vary significantly.

Concept

Given a list of six popular breakfast cereals the student should be able to list them according to their sugar content.

Objective

There are many sources of sucrose. Cereals comprise one group, the members of which contain significantly varying amounts of sucrose. Cereals are nutritious foods. They are even more nutritious eaten with milk. However, increasing the Calories in a food without concurrently increasing other nutrients, such as protein, vitamins, and minerals, tends to decrease its rating as a nutritious food. Many popular breakfast cereals contain added sugar (sucrose). Sucrose complicates the problem by being cariogenic (promoting tooth decay) in addition to adding unnecessary calories.

Nutrition Information

Cereals, consumed with milk as a meal or snack, are not the basis for concern, because the milk tends to wash the sucrose away from the teeth. However, a number of children eat presweetened cereals as a snack, especially while watching television. A presweetened cereal in this curriculum refers to any cereal that has a sweetener added during processing. Some of the familiar products used to presweeten cereals are sucrose, honey, corn syrup, invert sugar, and brown sugar. Many cereals containing a good deal of sweetener are not identifiable as having been sweetened. Some examples of presweetened cereals not identified as such are Trix, Golden Grahams, C. W. Post, Nature Valley Granola, Alpha-Bits, Apple-Jacks, Fruit Loops, and Fruity Pebbles.

The formation of a sticky mass against the teeth resulting from a continuing supply of sucrose presents a severe cariogenic condition. Since youngsters munch without thinking about the content of the food, this lesson is aimed at involving your students in some deliberate contemplation about the problem of high-sucrose foods. The relationship of eating habits and obesity is not considered here.

This lesson also provides practice in multiplication skills. Some of the values are decimal values, which may be rounded off to numbers your students can handle.

Note: Several days before the next lesson is to be taught, ask your students to save cereal boxes to be brought to class. If possible, one serving should remain in the box. You may wish to collect a supply for use by those students who neglect to bring their own cereal boxes. A couple of these boxes should be saved for use also in lesson 16.

Activity   This activity will take about one hour of student time.

Materials Needed
Cereals: Let's Look at Boxes
Sugar Content of Commercially Available Breakfast Cereals (a chart)
cereal boxes (with 1 serving [1 oz.] left in box)
bowls or paper cups (to hold single servings of cereals)
sugar cubes
index cards
masking tape
measuring cup

Part A
   The worksheet, Cereals: Let's Look at Boxes, should be completed individually by each student, who will use the box brought from home. However, findings should be compared in steps 4a, 4b, 7a, 7b, 7c, and 8. You may want to point out to students that the answers will vary, depending on which cereals were chosen. Computations begin in step 6; some students may need either your assistance or assistance from specified classmates.
   The chart, Sugar Content of Commercially Available Breakfast Cereals, lists the percentage of total sugar and sucrose in specific cereal products. If students have not been introduced to percentages and decimal fractions, you may want to tell them to think of the figure as "parts of one hundred." For example, 43 percent sucrose in Sugar Smacks may be described as 43 parts of sucrose in 100 parts. An illustration using 100 paper clips and separating 43 clips to represent sucrose content may also be helpful for some students.

Answer Key to Cereals: Let's Look at Boxes
1. through 4a. may be obtained directly from the box.
4b. may not be answered from the box directly. Following question 7c., students may answer this item.
5a. and 5b. may be obtained from the box.
6. through 7b. should be computed from cereal box date and the chart Sugar Content of Commercially Available Breakfast Cereals.
7c. The cereal with the most sucrose will be most likely to cause caries.
8. Students should find partners so that a presweetened cereal is compared to an unsweetened cereal. The first two columns require only information already obtained. Only the unsweetened cereal is to have .28 ounce of sucrose added. Depending on which two cereals are compared, either could be the one containing the most sucrose.
9. This item begins the preparation for the display. This series of computations might be good homework with which parents might be involved. For example:
   Sugar Smacks 43% sucrose
   1 oz serving × .43 = .43 oz. sucrose per serving
   1 oz = 7 tsps. sugar
   .43 × 7 = 3.01 tsp. sugar per serving

98

Part B

Paper cups will be needed. Students should follow step 9 in Cereals: Let's Look at Boxes. Cups should be labeled so that correct cereals may be matched with their respective sugar cube cups and empty boxes. A title banner should be made for the resource center—something like, "Think Before You Munch." A similar resource center will be used in a future lesson, in which foods other than cereals may be substituted. In each case, displayed foods should be arranged from lowest sucrose per serving to highest sucrose per serving. See illustration below.

A sample computation: Zoolies contain 75% sucrose

$$1 \text{ serving} = 1 \text{ ounce}$$

Pour enough cereal into the glass to make one serving.

1 ounce serving × .75 = .75 ounce sucrose per serving

1 ounce = 7 teaspoons

.75 × 7 = 5.25 teaspoons of sucrose per serving

rounded off, 5 sugar cubes (1 cube = 1 teaspoon sugar) should be placed in the other Zoolies' glass.

Check the computations on the worksheet for accuracy. You may also use the quiz items given below.

Evaluation

__c__ 1. Which cereal would you expect to have the most sucrose per serving?
   a. Shredded Wheat, large biscuit
   b. Shredded Wheat, spoon-size biscuits
   c. Frosted Mini Wheats
   d. Wheat Chex

__d__ 2. Which is the best statement about cereals?
   a. Cereals are not nutritious.
   b. Cereals have too much sugar for your teeth.
   c. All cereals make poor snacks.
   d. Some cereals have very little sucrose.

__a__ 3. If you didn't have a table to tell you how much sugar was in a cereal, how could you tell if it has a lot of sugar added to it?
   a. Sugar is one of the first ingredients listed.
   b. The number of calories per serving is low.
   c. The amount of fat is high.
   d. The amount of carbohydrate is high.

References
and
Resources

Films/Filmstrips
It's as Easy as Selling Candy to a Baby. 1977. Action for Children's
    Television, 46 Austin Street, Newtonville, MA 02160. Film, 16mm,
    color sound, 11 minutes. $25 (T)

Articles
Hayden, G. B. 1975. "Breakfast and Today's Lifestyles." *Journal of
    School Health* 45:83–87 (February). (T)
Liebman, B., and Perry, S. 1977. "Another Look at the 'Facts.'"
    Nutrition Action 7–12 (December). (T)
"USDA Analyzes Cereals for Five Food Sugars." 1979. *CNI Weekly* 9:7
    (July). (T)
"Which Cereals Are Most Nutritious?" 1975. *Consumer Reports* 76–82
    (February). (T)

Cereals: Let's Look at Boxes

Have you ever looked closely at the information on a cereal box? Look at your favorite cereal box and answer the following questions. Compare your answers to those of your classmates. You will probably be looking at a lot of different cereals.

1. What is the name of the cereal? _____

2. What is the manufacturer's name and address? _____
   _____

3. Look at the panel titled "Nutrition Information." It shows the amount of Iron CaPAC and other nutrients in this food. Cereals are often eaten with milk. Nutrition information is shown for the cereal alone and also for the cereal with milk.
   a. How many cereal servings are in this box? _____ Each serving weighs one ounce.
   b. How many Calories are there in one serving of this cereal (without milk)? _____
   c. How many grams of carbohydrate does a serving of this cereal without milk provide? _____ with milk? _____

4. Compare with your classmates:
   a. Which cereals are lower in carbohydrate? _____
      _____
   b. Are these lower in sucrose, too? (do not answer this until you've finished question #7) _____

5. Note the section headed *ingredients* on your cereal box. Ingredients are listed in order from the largest amount to the smallest amount.
   a. How many ingredients are listed? _____
   b. Where does sucrose fit into this listing? Look for the word *sugar*. First, second, third, fourth, fifth? _____

6. How can you compute the amount of sucrose in 1 serving of your cereal? To find out, see the example given below.
   Example: Sugar Smacks Cereal
   • The percentage of sucrose is *43%*
   (See the chart Sugar Content of Commercially Available Breakfast Cereals.)
   • The percentage changed to a decimal fraction is 43% x .01 = *.43*
   • The serving size of the cereal is *1 ounce*
   • Amount of sucrose in 1 serving is .43 x 1 ounce = *.43 ounce*

7. Compare the amount of sucrose in your cereal to the sucrose in a friend's cereal.
   a. Ounces of sucrose in one serving of your cereal _____
   b. Ounces of sucrose in one serving of your friend's cereal _____
   c. Which cereal is less likely to cause cavities? _____

8. If you put two teaspoons of sugar on a serving of nonpresweetened cereal, would it have as much sucrose as a presweetened cereal? To find out, complete the following table (*Note*: 1 teaspoon equals about .14 ounce.)

Cereal Name	% sucrose in cereal	ounces sucrose + in cereal	weight in ounces of 2 tsp. of = added sugar	Total ounces of sugar
(presweetened)			none	
(nonpresweetened)			.28	

Which cereal has the most sucrose per serving?_____

Compare your answer with at least three other students.

9. Now you are ready to prepare your display of cereal sucrose content.

   a. You will need two paper bowls or cups. They should be the same size. Put a masking-tape label on each glass. Each label should show the name of your cereal.

   b. You will measure only one serving of your cereal. Your serving will be placed in one of your glasses.

   c. Now show how much sucrose is in a serving of your cereal. Let one sugar cube represent one teaspoon of sucrose. You can compute the number of sugar cubes this way: (Your teacher will explain.)

   _____ x _____ = _____

   ounces of sucrose in a serving (see #6) | teaspoons of sugar in an ounce | teaspoons of sucrose in a serving

   Teaspoons of sucrose in a serving is the same number as the number of sugar cubes you will need. Round the number off to the nearest whole cube. How many sugar cubes should you put in your glass? _____

   d. You are now ready to add your cereal, serving glass, and sugar cube glass to the class display. Your teacher will tell you where to place them.

Sugar Content of Commercially Available Breakfast Cereals

Product	Total Sugar (%)	Sucrose (%)	Product	Total Sugar (%)	Sucrose (%)
Sugar Smacks	56	43	Raisin Bran (K)	29	11
Apple Jacks	54.6	54	C. W. Post Raisins	29	18
Fruit Loops	48	48	C. W. Post	28.7	20
Raisin Bran (GF)	48	11	Frosted Mini Wheats	26	26
Sugar Corn Pops	46	39	Country Crisp	22	18
Super Sugar Crisp	46	36	Life, Cinnamon	21	21
Crazy Cow, chocolate	45.6	42	100% Bran	21	19
Corny Snaps	45.5	45	All Bran	19	16
Frosted Rice Krinkies	44	43.3	Fortified Oat Flakes	18.5	18
Frankenberry	43.7	38	Life	16	16
Cookie Crisp, vanilla	43.5	43	Team	14.1	12
Cap'n Crunch, Crunch Berries	43.3	42	40% Bran	13	10
Cocoa Krispies	43	41	Grape Nuts Flakes	13.3	7
Cocoa Pebbles	42.6	42	Buckwheat	12.2	10
Fruity Pebbles	42.5	42	Product 19	9.9	8.1
Lucky Charms	42.2	36	Concentrate	9.3	9
Cookie Crisp, chocolate	41	40	Total	8.3	.7
Sugar Frosted Flakes of Corn	41	39	Wheaties	8.2	7
Quisp	40.7	40	Rice Krispies	7.8	7
Crazy Cow, strawberry	40.1	38	Grape Nuts	7	ND
Cookie Crisp, oatmeal	40.1	39	Special K	5.4	5
Cap'n Crunch	40	40	Corn Flakes	5.3	3
Count Chocula	39.5	35	Post Toasties	5	3
Alpha Bits	38	38	Kix	4.8	4
Honey Comb	37.2	37	Rice Chex	4.4	4
Frosted Rice	37	35	Corn Chex	4	4
Trix	35.9	33	Wheat Chex	3.5	2
Cocoa Puffs	33.3	32	Cheerios	3	3
Cap'n Crunch, Peanut Butter	32.2	32	Shredded Wheat	0.6	0.6
Golden Grahams	30	27	Puffed Wheat	0.5	0.5
Cracklin' Bran	29	27	Puffed Rice	0.1	0.1

- Letter in parentheses following the product refers to the manufacturer: GF = General Foods; K = Kellogg's
- ND = not detected

Lesson 16
Snack Plaque Fighters I

Health

Like fat, sugar also hides in many foods.

Concepts

   Except for fresh fruits and natural juices, snacks with hidden sugar are not good for the teeth.

Given a list of snack foods, the student should be able to identify which foods contain hidden sugar.

Objective

The student should know that snacks chosen wisely can contribute significantly to the total nutritional intake for a day. For example, a glass of milk is a good-to-excellent source of several nutrients: calcium, phosphorus, protein, vitamins A and D, riboflavin. Lean meat is a good source of protein as well as iron and several B vitamins. Citrus fruits are rich in vitamin C. These nutrients and others are essential for proper development of teeth and gums and the supporting structures of the jaw.

Nutrition Information

   On the other hand, snacks that list sugar (sucrose) and its various forms (corn syrup or sweeteners, glucose, honey, invert sugar, brown sugar) as the main ingredient are poor source, of protein, vitamins, and minerals. The word "sugar" on an ingredient label refers only to its sucrose (table sugar) content. Molasses and brown sugar are composed chiefly of sucrose too. Corn syrup, invert sugar, and honey are chiefly composed of fructose or glucose. All of these simple sugars have been found to be associated with dental caries. However, sucrose is often cited as the most cariogenic. Therefore, snacks high in simple sugar (especially sucrose) that provide little nutritional value other than Calories should be limited. The table, Hidden Sugar in Foods (Appendix H), provides information on the sugar content of several foods containing added sugar. For many of the foods shown, sucrose is usually the sugar present in greater amounts (jam, jelly, and some fruit drinks often have corn syrup as their main sugar).

   Briefly, sugar plays the following role in dental disease. 1) The bacteria found in the mouth feed on sugar. In turn, the bacteria produce a sticky substance called plaque that adheres to the teeth and gums. 2) Bacteria then make their home in the plaque. Here they ingest sugar and produce an acid. Exposure of the teeth to this acid over a period of time causes dental caries (decay). 3) Plaque and the resultant acid can cause inflammation of the gums (gingivitis) and eventually periodontal disease. An overabundance of high sugar-content snacks may also lead to dietary deficiencies of vitamins and minerals as well as excessive gains in body fat.

Although fresh fruits contain sucrose as one of three simple sugars, the concentration is relatively low. However, canned and frozen fruits can be more orally hazardous if sugar has been added. Dried fruits, which have had the water removed, contain concentrated sucrose. The water and fiber content of many fresh fruits and vegetables (apples, carrots, and celery) can aid in flushing and cleansing the teeth.

Research indicates that the physical form of food, foodstuff remaining in the mouth, and the frequency of between-meal snacks are of more significance in tooth decay than the quantity of sugar ingested.

For example, look at the two sample diets. The quantity and selection of foods is identical. However, Diet 2 is more cariogenic than Diet 1. The frequency of sugar contact with the teeth is higher in Diet 2.

	Diet 1	Diet 2
Breakfast	½ cup orange juice *1 ounce Frosted Flakes ½ cup milk *1 sweet roll	½ cup orange juice *1 ounce Frosted Flakes ½ cup milk
Mid-Morning Snack		*1 sweet roll
Lunch	*1 cup chocolate milk 1 tuna sandwich *1 cookie (2½ inches dia.) *2 dates	*1 cup chocolate milk 1 tuna sandwich 4 carrot sticks
Afternoon Snack 1		*1 cookie (2½ inches dia.)
Afternoon Snack 2	4 carrot sticks	*dates
Frequency of sugar contact	2	5

*considered to be orally hazardous

The following groups of snacks are generally considered orally safe:
• white milk, buttermilk, cottage cheese, all other cheeses, cheese and sour cream dips, plain yogurt;
• leftover meats, hard cooked eggs, nuts, bean dip, tacos, pizza, hamburgers, cheeseburgers, hot dogs, peanut butter without sugar added;
• buttered popcorn, saltine or soda crackers;
• sour or dill pickles, olives, sugarless gum, beverages (other than white milk) which do not have sugar added.
Snacks generally considered to be hazardous to oral health and that should therefore be limited include: candy, cake, cookies, pies, doughnuts, pastries; honey, jelly, jam, syrup; dry, ready-to-eat presweetened breakfast cereals, soft drinks; and regular and bubble gum, breath mints, and cough drops.

Activity   The activity in this lesson makes students aware of foods containing added or hidden sugar in serving sizes of specific foods. The activity in the next lesson presents other factors to consider in determining the degree to which specific foods are diets are orally hazardous.

Materials Needed
Hidden Sugar in Foods (Appendix H)
containers (empty or full) of as many of the foods as possible, listed in
  Appendix H
pictures of foods listed in Appendix H
sugar cubes
pencils or pens and paper

Part A
  Without any discussion of snacks, have the students list their ten
favorite snacks and place them along a continuum from most sugar to
no sugar. Following Part B, have the students review their list of snacks
and make corrections as needed.

Part B
  The object of Part B is for students to learn how much added or
hidden sugar is present in certain foods. To visualize this, the student will
work at a resource center designed by you.
  Explain to students that many foods have sugar added to them before
we purchase them. White table sugar (sucrose) is often added as well as
other sugars (corn syrup, invert sugar, and dextrose).
  For foods listed on the chart Hidden Sugar in Foods that you have no
containers for, have students cut out pictures or draw them. The students
should then mark the number of teaspoons of sugar per serving of food
(as shown on the chart) on each picture or container. In a central
location, place together the containers and pictures of food, along with a
box of sugar cubes. Now have the students make a display showing the
amount of sugar in each of the foods. Usually one sugar cube equals a
teaspoon of sugar, but check the box to be sure. Discuss their reactions
to the hidden sugar in foods and conclude with the following points:
• Sugar-containing foods such as candy, cakes, soda pop, pie, and
cookies are considered to be orally hazardous snacks.
• Dried fruits, such as dates and raisins, are also not good snacks for
teeth.
• Besides the amount of added or hidden sugar in a food, there are
other factors to consider in determining how orally hazardous a food is.
The next lesson will help us learn about these other factors.
  If time allows, you may want to have students look at ingredient labels
on the containers and identify the different kinds of sugar present. Keep
this resource center intact for the next lesson.

Materials Needed   Alternate Activity
Plaque Fighter Food Record (Appendix I)
Hidden Sugar in Foods (Appendix H)

  In this activity each student should record on the food record
everything eaten for a forty-eight-hour period. Be sure that students read
and understand the instructions before the information is collected.
  Using the chart Hidden Sugar in Foods, have the students evaluate
their food record by noting the frequency of sucrose-containing foods
consumed each day.

Upon completion of this lesson, students should review the list of their   Evaluation
ten favorite snacks placed along the continuum from most orally
hazardous to most orally safe. They should make corrections in their

placement of these snacks to make the continuum accurate.

You may also decide to use the quiz items given below.

__b__ 1. Which of the following snack foods is not orally hazardous?
        a. pie
        b. popcorn
        c. cookies
        d. donuts

__c__ 2. Which of the following foods has the least amount of sugar?
        a. ½ cup of ice cream
        b. a cup of chocolate milk
        c. one whole carrot
        d. a piece of chocolate cake

References and Resources

Books

Abisch, R., and Kaplan, B. 1976. *The Munchy, Crunchy, Healthy Kid's Snack Book.* New York: Walker and Co. $6.50 (S)

Pamphlets

"Diet and Dental Health." No date. American Dental Association, 211 East Chicago Avenue, Chicago, IL 60611. $3.30/25 (T)

"Research Explores Nutrition and Dental Health." 1970. Superintendent of Documents, U.S. Government Printing Office, Washington, D.C. 20402. DHEW Publication No. (NIH) 74-647. 40¢ (T)

Posters

"Nutrition Sports Mobile." 1977. Sunkist Growers, Consumer Services Dept., P.O. Box 7888, Van Nuys, CA 91409. Free. (S)

"Relax with an Apple." 1974. International Apple Institute, 2430 Pennsylvania Avenue, NW, Washington, D.C. 20037. Free. (S)

Films/Filmstrips

Merlin's Magical Message. 1976. Modern Talking Picture Service, 1212 Avenue of the Americas, New York, NY 10036. Film, color, 6 minutes. Free loan. (S)

Showdown at Sweet Rock Gulch. 1975. Modern Talking Picture Service, 1212 Avenue of the Americas, New York, NY 10036. Film, color, 10 minutes. Free loan. (S)

Too Much of a Good Thing? Marsh Film Enterprises, P.O. Box 8082, Shawnee Mission, KS 66208. Filmstrip/record, teaching guide. $22.50 (S)

Articles

Chamberlain, A. D. H. 1977. "Diet and Dental Health." *Life and Health* 30–31 (October). (T)

McNutt, K. W. 1976. "Perspective: Fiber." *Journal of Nutrition Education* 8:150–52 (October–December). (T)

Navia, J. M. 1979. "Nutrition, Diet, and Oral Health." *Food and Nutrition News* 50:1–4 (February). (T)

"Nutrition and Oral Health." 1978. *Dairy Council Digest* 49 (May–June). (T)

Lesson 17
Snack Plaque Fighters II

Mathematics

Interdisciplinary Emphasis

Sticky-sweet foods are the most orally hazardous. Snacking on sucrose-containing foods throughout the day is more orally hazardous than eating these foods at mealtime. Examples of snacks that are orally safe include fresh fruits and vegetables, unsweetened juices, milk, cheese, and nuts.

Concepts

Given food pairs, groups and sample diets, students will identify:
* which foods are the most orally hazardous;
* which diet is the most orally hazardous;
* which foods are orally safe.

Objective

Refer to Lesson 16.

Nutrition Information

If you did the alternate activity in the last lesson, you will not have a resource center prepared (required in this lesson's activity). Therefore, do the alternate activity in this lesson, unless you want to go back and construct the resource center.

Activity

Materials Needed
"Hidden Sugar in Food" display constructed in previous lesson
Healthful Snacks

Part A
  While viewing the resource center constructed in the previous lesson, students should identify which foods they feel are the most orally hazardous. An effective way to do this is to pull out two or three foods at a time from the center and have students identify the most orally hazardous in each case. Good examples follow, with the most orally hazardous food asterisked (*) in each case.
* Apple Butter (1T); *Jelly or Jam (1T)
* 7-Up (8 ounces); Cola (8 ounces); *Plain Chocolate Cake (1 piece)
* Chocolate Milk (8 ounces); *Glazed Doughnut (1)
* *Ginger Snap (1); Tapioca Pudding (½ cup)
* *Gum Drops (¼ package); Pumpkin Pie (1 slice)
Make sure to discuss the reason each food is identified as the most

orally hazardous. Lead students to the following conclusions.
- When you determine how orally hazardous sucrose-containing foods are, the physical form of the food is more important than the amount of sucrose in the foods.
- If the physical form of sucrose-containing foods is the same, the food with the most sucrose in it should be considered the most orally hazardous.
- If the physical form of sucrose-containing foods is different, the food that sticks to the teeth the longest is the most orally hazardous.

With the students, identify other examples of sticky-sweet foods.

Part B

The Nutrition Information in the previous lesson illustrates two diets, both containing exactly the same orally hazardous foods. Either on the blackboard or on a transparency, show this diet to the students. Have them identify the orally hazardous foods in each diet (you should circle them). Then, have the students vote on the following options:

1) "How many of you think that *Diet 1* is just as bad for the teeth as *Diet 2?*"
2) "How many of you think that one of these diets is more orally hazardous than the other?"

One or two students who voted for option 1 should be called on to support why they voted this way. Repeat this for option 2.

Diet 2 is obviously the most orally hazardous because the frequency of sugar contacts with the teeth is greater (5 versus 2). This concept could probably be grasped best by epxlaining that the more separate times you ingest sucrose-containing foods throughout the day, the more orally hazardous your diet is. This is partly because sugar is in your mouth more often. Go through Diet 1 and Diet 2, counting the sugar contacts in each, establishing that Diet 2 is the more orally hazardous.

Announce that a future lesson (19) will further illustrate why it is better to eat sucrose-containing foods at mealtime than to snack on them throughout the day.

Part C

Summarize the factors involved in determining how orally hazardous a diet is:

1) The number of orally hazardous (sucrose-containing) foods in the diet.
2) The number of these orally hazardous foods that are sticky or that adhere to the teeth.
3) Whether the orally hazardous foods are eaten at mealtime or snacked on throughout the day.

Have students individually identify what they consider to be "orally safe" snacks for the following situations:

- When fruit or juice snacks are wanted.
- When a drink is wanted.
- When crunchy food is wanted.
- When a "filling" snack is wanted, that is, a snack to satisfy a big hunger.

Distribute the worksheet Healthful Snacks to the students and have them check their answers. Students should be encouraged to identify snacks they believe are orally safe that are not listed on the worksheet. If you wish, students could also make a Healthful Snacks poster or handout for younger children.

110

Materials Needed
Hidden Sugar in Food (Appendix H)
Plaque Fighters Food Record (Appendix I)

   Follow the same procedures given in the activity in this lesson, but in Part A, have students work directly from the chart Hidden Sugars in Foods rather than from the resource center.
   Additionally, if students completed the forty-eight-hour food record in the alternate activity from the previous lesson, you might follow up Part B by having students count the number of sugar contacts in each twenty-four-hour period and compare with other students' records, an activity that would reveal ways to make their diets more orally safe.

__d__ 1. Which food below would be the most orally hazardous?
   a. root beer
   b. chocolate milk
   c. ice cream
   d. caramels

__a__ 2. John snacked on orally hazardous foods throughout the day. Jim ate the same number of orally hazardous foods, but he ate them at mealtimes. Whose diet is the most orally hazardous?
   a. John's
   b. Jim's
   c. both diets are equally hazardous
   d. neither diet would be hazardous

__c__ 3. Which food would be the least orally hazardous?
   a. glazed doughnut
   b. chocolate mints
   c. chocolate milk
   d. gum drops

__b__ 4. Which food would be the least orally safe?
   a. popcorn
   b. ginger snap cookie
   c. carrot
   d. cheese

Pamphlets
"A Review: Nutrition, Diet, and the Teeth." United Fresh Fruit and Vegetable Association, 1019 Nineteenth Street, NW, Washington, D.C. 20036. Reprint. 40¢ (T)

Posters
"Do You?" 1967. National Dairy Council, 6300 N. River Road, Rosemont, IL 60018. Poster, teacher's guide. 40¢ (S)
"Have a Happy Healthy Smile!" 1978. National Dairy Council, 6300 N. River Road, Rosemont, IL 60018. 40¢ (S)
"Nutrition Sports Mobile." 1977. Sunkist Growers, Consumer Services Dept., P.O. Box 7888, Van Nuys, CA 91409. Free. (S)

Films/Filmstrips
Toothtown, USA. 1975. National Dairy Council, 6300 N. River Road, Rosemont, IL 60018. Filmstrip/audiocassette, leader's guide, 16mm, color, 20 minutes each side. $20 (S)

Articles

Edgar, W. M.; Bibby, B. G.; Mundorff, S., and Rowley, J. 1975. "Acid Production in Plaques After Eating Snacks: Modifying Factors in Foods." *Journal of the American Dietetic Association* 90:418–25 (February). (T)

Madsen, K. O. 1975. "Frequency of Eating and Dental Health." *Food and Nutrition News* 46:1–4 (March–April). (T)

Stahler, E. 1979. "A Nation Sweet on Sugar." *Nutrition Action* 9–12 (August). (T)

Learning Packet

"Learning About Your Oral Health, Level Two." 1973. American Dental Association, 211 East Chicago Avenue, Chicago, IL 69611. Overhead transparencies, spirit masters, booklets. $4 (S)

Healthful Snacks

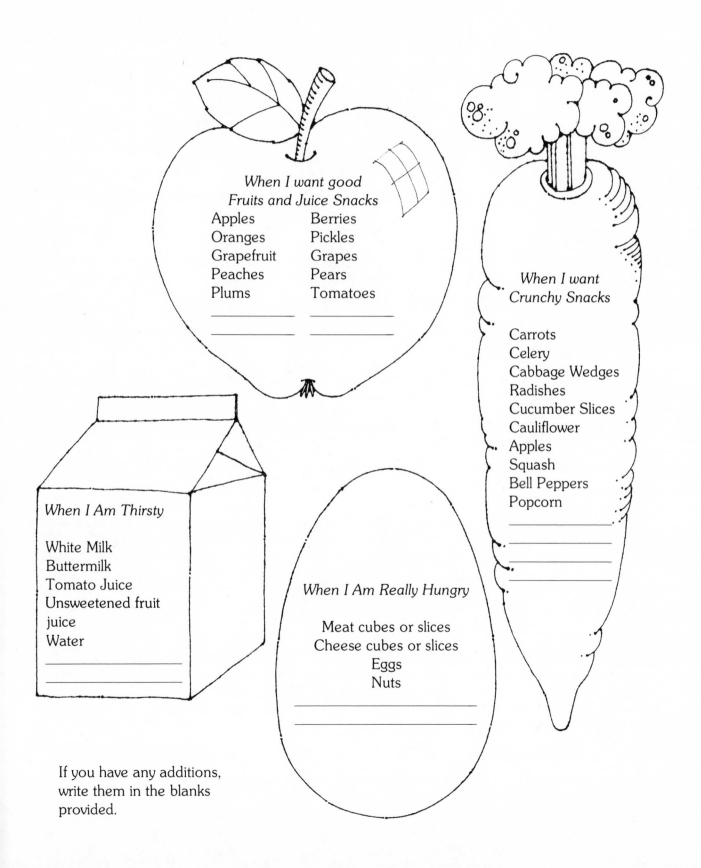

When I want good
Fruits and Juice Snacks

Apples	Berries
Oranges	Pickles
Grapefruit	Grapes
Peaches	Pears
Plums	Tomatoes

_____ _____

_____ _____

*When I want
Crunchy Snacks*

Carrots
Celery
Cabbage Wedges
Radishes
Cucumber Slices
Cauliflower
Apples
Squash
Bell Peppers
Popcorn

_____

_____

_____

When I Am Thirsty

White Milk
Buttermilk
Tomato Juice
Unsweetened fruit
juice
Water

_____

_____

When I Am Really Hungry

Meat cubes or slices
Cheese cubes or slices
Eggs
Nuts

_____

_____

If you have any additions,
write them in the blanks
provided.

Lesson 18
Bacteria

Science Interdisciplinary Emphasis

Bacteria are microscopic and, like man, use the nutrients in food.

Concepts

After completing the worksheets in this lesson, students should be able to: 1) define microorganisms, 2) list two ways microorganisms help us and two ways microorganisms hurt us, and 3) list five methods of food preservation that slow microbial growth.

Objective

Microorganisms, such as bacteria, yeast, and fungi, no doubt outnumber other living things on this earth and are found virtually everywhere. These microscopic organisms are also called *microbes* and are eventually responsible for the final decomposition of plant and animal material. They can grow on the human food supply, using the nutrients there for their growth. Therefore, man has had to learn to control the growth of these microorganisms in order to protect his food. Cooking, refrigerating, freezing, drying, salting, smoking, canning, sterilizing, pasteurizing, and adding certain preservative substances (nitrites and calcium propionate) are processes man has used to prevent microbial contamination of his food.

Nutrition Information

Microorganisms were not identified as the agents contributing to food spoilage until a century ago. However, wine, cheese, and bread were unknowingly made with the help of these living organisms for at least two thousand years. Many microorganisms are still used today by man to flavor and preserve his foods. Yeast is used for making bread, beer, and wine. Microorganisms added to milk produce dairy products such as cheese, yogurt, and buttermilk.

This lesson emphasizes the dual role of microorganisms: certain kinds *hurt* man by causing food spoilage while other kinds *help* man by preserving and flavoring foods.

Materials Needed
Questions and Answers on Microorganisms
biology text (optional)
microscope (optional)
prepared slides of dyed yeast cells (optional)
3 glass jars with lids

Activity

warm water (115–120°F)
1 package dry yeast
½ cup flour
2 Tbsp. sugar
measuring spoons

You may wish to prepare the three jars used in Part B before completing the reading in Part A. If you do, make sure students observe as you prepare them.

Part A

With students, read aloud and discuss Questions and Answers on Microorganisms. Since a part of the reading deals with temperatures in both Centigrade and Fahrenheit, you may wish to spend some time illustrating (or reviewing) how to convert from one scale to the other ($°F=9/5°C+32$) ($°C=5/9 [°F–32]$)

Part B

Your role in this activity is to illustrate how microorganisms, like man, are dependent on nutrients found in food to grow.

In jar one place 1 tsp. of the dry yeast.

In jar two place 1 tsp. dry yeast and ½ cup of warm water. Close the jar and shake to mix well.

In jar three place 1 tsp. dry yeast, ¼ cup flour, 2 Tbsp. sugar, and 1 cup warm water. Close the jar and shake to mix well.

If you wish you may select groups of students to prepare the jars one at a time. Let the three prepared jars sit in a warm place for 20 minutes. Jar three should exhibit yeast growth as evidenced by the foam. The other two jars should show little or no evidence of yeast growth because of the lack of sufficient nutrients to promote growth.

You may want to relate jar three to the bread-baking process. The carbon dioxide produced by the yeast is trapped by the dough. The result is a light, airy product. Ask students the following thought questions concerning jar three.

1. What happens to bread dough after it has been allowed to sit in a warm place? (The dough rises.)
2. What is responsible for the growth? (The yeast produces the gas, carbon dioxide, which is trapped by the dough.)

If you have the time and the resources, you may want to have students view pictures of yeast and other microorganisms in biology texts. You may want them to view dyed yeast cells through a microscope.

Evaluation

<u>c</u> 1. Microorganisms are small living cells that require _____ for growth.
   a. air
   b. darkness
   c. nutrients
   d. temperatures below 40°F.

<u>b</u> 2. Food is the only carrier of microorganisms.
   a. true
   b. false

<u>c</u> 3. A sterile environment
   a. favors the growth of microorganisms.
   b. favors the growth of yeast and molds.
   c. is a clean environment.
   d. is kept above 140°F.

116

<u> a </u> 4. Foods stay fresher longer in a refrigerator because
     a. the temperature inside the refrigerator is below 40°F.
     b. the dark environment does not favor mold growth.
     c. the air circulating inside the refrigerator is sterile.
     d. the moisture present in the circulating air is very low.

<u> d </u> 5. The "danger zone" of food refers to
     a. the temperatures at which microorganisms grow best.
     b. 40°F to 114°F.
     c. none of the above.
     d. both a. & b.

Food processing can limit the growth of microorganisms. List five methods of food preservation that slow down the growth of microorganisms.

6. (drying)
7. (salting)
8. (smoking)
9. (freezing)
10. (canning) (pasteurizing) (sterilizing) (additives)

Books

References and Resources

Carona, P. B. 1975. *Chemistry and Cooking.* Englewood Cliffs, N.J.: Prentice-Hall. $5.95 (S)

Cobb, V. 1972. *Science Experiments You Can Eat.* Philadelphia: J.B. Lippincott Co. $4.95 (S)

Hertzberg, R.; Vaughan, B.; and Greene, J. 1975. *Putting Food By.* 2d ed. Brattleboro, Vt.: Stephen Greene Press. $4.95 (T)

Labuza, T. 1977. *Food and Your Well-Being.* St. Paul: West Publishing Co. $9.95 (T)

Mayer, C. 1971. *The Bread Book.* New York: Harcourt Brace Jovanovich. $6.95 (S)

Nester, E. W.; Roberts, C. F.; McCarthy, B. J.; and Pearsall, N. N. 1973. *Microbiology.* New York: Holt, Rinehart, and Winston. $19.95 (T)

Pamphlets

"Keeping Food Safe." 1975. Superintendent of Documents, U.S. Government Printing Office, Washington, D.C. 20402. Home and Garden Bulletin No. 162, Stock No. 001-000-03396-4. 30¢ (T)

Booklets

"Ball Blue Book, the Guide to Home Canning and Freezing." 1977. Ball Corporation, Muncie, IN. $2.50 (T)

"Handbook of Food Preparation." 7th ed. 1975. American Home Economics Association, 2010 Massachusetts Avenue, NW, Washington, D.C. 20036. $4 (T)

Posters

"If It's Cold, Keep It Cold!" 1976. U.S. Food and Drug Administration, U.S. Government Printing Office, Washington, D.C. 20402. U.S. Dept. of Health, Education and Welfare Publication No. (FDA) 74-2068. 35¢ (S,T)

Films/Filmstrips

Complete Teaching Kit on Cheese. No date. Kraft Foods Educational Dept., 500 Peshtigo Court, Chicago, IL 60690. Two filmstrips/ teacher's guide, 35mm, three transparencies, wall chart. $12 (S)

It's Good Food; Keep It Safe. No date (ca. 1972). U.S. Extension Service, U.S. Dept. of Agriculture, Washington, D.C. 20250. Four filmstrips/two phonodiscs, 16mm, filmstrip keys. Free. (S,T)

Let's Keep Food Safe to Eat. 1964. Coronet Instructional Films, Coronet Building, 65 E. South Water Street, Chicago, IL 60601. Film, 16mm, color, sound, 11 minutes. $130 (S,T)

Articles

"The High Filth Diet, Compliments of FDA." 1973. *The FDA* 152–54 (March). (T)

Zottola, E. A. 1977. "Food-Borne Disease I." *Contemporary Nutrition* 2 (September). (T)

Questions and Answers on Microorganisms

Q: *What are microorganisms?*

A: Microorganisms are very, very small living cells that can be seen only under a microscope. Bacteria, yeast, fungi, microbes, and "germs" are some of the names used for microorganisms.

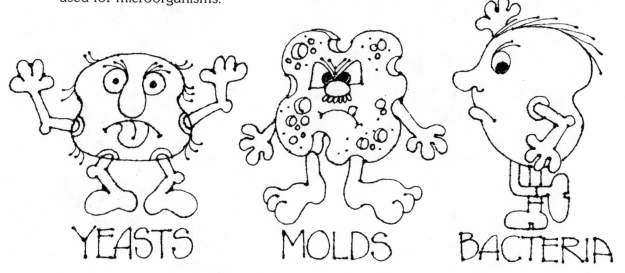

Q: *What do microorganisms need for growth?*

A: Microorganisms need a favorable environment. Like man, they need nutrients, water, and the right temperature. Some also need darkness. Not all of them need air. Some can grow in canned foods where there is no air.

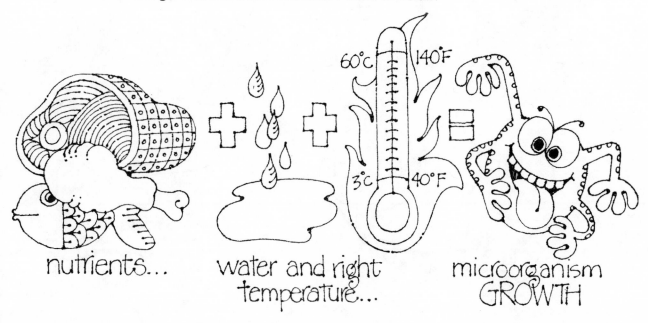

nutrients...   water and right temperature...   microorganism GROWTH

Q: *How can the growth of microorganisms in food be controlled?*

A: Food may be protected from the growth of microorganisms if the environment of the food is not favorable.

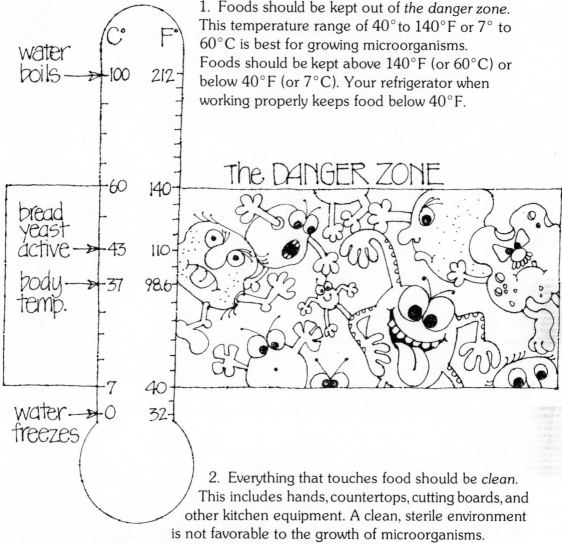

1. Foods should be kept out of *the danger zone.* This temperature range of 40° to 140°F or 7° to 60°C is best for growing microorganisms. Foods should be kept above 140°F (or 60°C) or below 40°F (or 7°C). Your refrigerator when working properly keeps food below 40°F.

2. Everything that touches food should be *clean.* This includes hands, countertops, cutting boards, and other kitchen equipment. A clean, sterile environment is not favorable to the growth of microorganisms.

3. Processing foods also limits the growth of microorganisms.

   drying: Food that has been dried limits the growth of microorganisms because they need moisture.

   salting: Salting prevents microorganisms from getting enough water to grow.

   smoking: Smoking adds substances to foods that slow the growth of microorganisms. The processes of drying and salting are usually done before smoking the food.

   freezing: Microorganisms will not grow if it is too *cold.* Freezing food also "locks up" the water and makes it unavailable for their growth.

   canning, pasteurizing, sterilizing: Microorganisms are killed with high temperatures. These are three *hot* ways to preserve and protect food from their growth.

   additives: Sometimes substances are added to food to preserve and protect it. For example, calcium propionate is a chemical additive which is used in bread products to prevent the growth of mold.

Lesson 19
Plaque, Acid, and Teeth

Health

Bacteria, living in plaque on our teeth, turn sugar (especially sucrose) into acid. This acid is harmful to the teeth, causing cavities.

The student should 1) define the term *plaque* as a mass of bacteria and sugar which sticks to teeth; and 2) explain the relationship between dental cavities and plaque: plaque plus sugar yields acid; acid acting on enamel of teeth develops cavities.

Plaque is primarily a colony of colorless and sticky bacteria. It may become stained by food and is directly attached to the teeth. The bacteria, which are a part of plaque, feed on simple sugars and produce a sticky substance called dextran. The plaque is held onto the tooth by the dextran. Caries (cavities) form in those zones on the teeth where plaque is present. Certain kinds of bacteria that live in the plaque feed on simple sugars and may not be the same ones that produce dextran. Millions of bacteria are in each person's mouth. They may be free (unorganized) or held together (organized) in a plaque formation. Although the unorganized bacteria produce some acid, this acid does not appreciably contribute to the production of caries. The organized bacteria trapped in the plaque react with simple sugar that is placed in the mouth and produce acid. This acid is held to the tooth by plaque and produces caries.

  Some acids dissolve calcium compounds on the teeth, causing caries. Others break down connective tissues, causing periodontal (gum) disease.

This activity will require an hour or more of student time.

Materials Needed

toothpicks	water
clean glass slides	jar
methyl red (0.2% aqueous solution)	litmus paper
sugar cubes	paper
dry yeast	pens

  Students should complete experiment A, B, or C. If you have time, you may wish to have the students complete all three experiments.

Interdisciplinary Emphasis

Concepts

Objective

Nutrition Information

Activity

Experiment A:

Step 1. Have the students scrape plaque from between their teeth near the gum line with the use of a toothpick.

Step 2. Put the plaque on a clean glass slide and arrange it into a circle of ¼ inch diameter, like a doughnut. (You may want to have each student prepare two slides, omitting step 4 on the slide serving as a control.)

Step 3. Add two drops of methyl red (0.2% aqueous solution) to cover the mass. (Color should be noted.)

Step 4. Add a few crystals of sugar to the liquid in the center of the ring. Those students whose bacteria form acid rapidly will instantly see a red color on the sugar crystals, indicating acid production. (Color should be noted.)

Experiment B: This experiment is an example of acid production by "organized" bacteria.

Step 1. Give half a lump of sugar to each member of a group of students to eat at the beginning of class. Have them get the concentrated sugar on the teeth near the gum line. (Again, you may want to designate a comparison group of students who do not get the sugar, but rather rinse their mouths well with water.)

Step 2. Place the methyl red on the teeth directly and watch the red color develop, indicating the presence of acid. (If you set up a comparison group, apply methyl red as described above and watch for red color. Observe differences between the groups.)

Step 3. Have students report their experimental results. An example of a report sheet is given below. You may want to place it on the blackboard for students to copy.

Plaque, Bacteria, and Acid

Name _____ Date _____
Experiment: _____
What I did: _____ (several lines) _____
What I observed: _____ (several lines) _____
Reasoning: _____ (several lines) _____

Experiment C: This experiment is an example of acid production by "free" or "unorganized" bacteria.

Step 1. Students combine sugar, yeast, and water in a jar. Immediately, test for acid with litmus paper and record results.

Step 2. After about four days, the students again test for acid with litmus paper and record results. What color was the litmus before and after it was put into the yeast? (The yeast in this experiment is acting like bacteria in our mouths.)

Step 3. Have the students report their experimental results. An example of a report sheet is given below. You may want to place it on the blackboard for students to copy.

Report Form Experiment C

Name _____ Date _____
A. *Procedure:* (Tell what you've done to make the mixture. Name the ingredients and state amounts of each used.)
_____ (several lines) _____

B. *Predictions:* If yeast, like the bacteria in our mouth, produces acid, the blue litmus paper will appear
_____ (color)

C. *Observations:* Tell what happened when you tested with the litmus paper.
Day 1 _____ (several lines) _____
Day 4 _____ (several lines) _____
What color does acid turn blue litmus paper? _____

The write-up of the experiments should be evaluated for clarity in explaining the experiment and the reasoning behind it.
    The following set of equations involving the plaque process can also be used as an evaluation tool.

Evaluation

Directions:
    Use the terms listed below to complete this chart on the plaque process.

_____ + _____ = ___ plaque ___
_____ + _____ = ___ acid ___
_____ + _____ = ___ cavities ___

Scrambled terms to use in equations:

retiacab _____   gusra _____
cadi _____   tthoo _____
quaple _____

Answers to equations:

bacteria	+	sugar	=	plaque
plaque	+	sugar	=	acid
acid	+	tooth	=	cavities

Sample quiz items are also given here:

__c__ 1. What is plaque?
    a. a wire attached to the tooth
    b. an instrument used to clean the teeth
    c. a sticky mass of bacteria on the teeth
    d. a food that is not good for us

__c__ 2. What holds acid to the tooth surface?
    a. sweet, sticky foods
    b. bacteria
    c. plaque
    d. calculus

__a__ 3. When sweet, sticky foods are in your mouth, bacteria in plaque produce:
    a. acid
    b. mold
    c. yeast
    d. juice

Pamphlets
"Break the Chain of Tooth Decay." No date. American Dental Association, 211 East Chicago Avenue, Chicago, IL 60611. First copy free/bulk rates available. (S,T)

References and Resources

Posters
"Kick the Sweet Snack Habit." 1975. American Dental Association, 211 East Chicago Avenue, Chicago, IL 60611. Chart. $2.95/100 (S,T)

125

Films/Filmstrips
Diet and Dental Health. 1974. American Dietetic Association, 430 N.
Michigan Avenue, Chicago, IL 60611. Audiotape/study guide, 50
minutes. $11 ADA members/$16 nonmembers. (T)

Learning Packet
"Learning About Your Oral Health: Prevention-Oriented School
Program." 1975. American Dental Association, Order Section BD-83,
211 East Chicago Avenue, Chicago, IL 60611. Level II Teaching
Packet. $1.97 (T)

Lesson 20
Protein: First a Builder

Mathematics

The body uses protein mainly as building blocks for growth and the repair of body tissue.

Concepts

    Protein can also be used for energy. Protein supplies as much energy as carbohydrate but less than half as much as fat.

Given background information, students should be able to determine:
1) when protein is used for building tissue and when it is not; and
2) the Caloric value of a food from its protein, carbohydrate, and fat composition.

Objective

Protein is a Greek word which means primary or holding first place. This definition describes the important role dietary protein plays in nutrition. In this lesson the role of dietary protein will be discussed only briefly.

Nutrition Information

    The primary role of dietary protein is to provide amino acids, which in turn are used to build enzymes, hormones, and body tissues. In two previous lessons protein was mentioned as an energy source. Amino acids are used for energy when an insufficiency of dietary carbohydrate or fat occurs. Amino acids in excess of the body's building needs are also used for energy or are converted to fat and stored as potential energy. Thus, we say that the secondary role of protein is to supply energy to the body. Use of protein for energy is a waste of its tissue- and enzyme-building potential.

    When used for energy, protein supplies 4 Calories per gram; this is the same amount that carbohydrate supplies but less than one-half as much as fat (9 Calories per gram). A cup of whole milk contains all three of the energy-yielding nutrients:

        7.3 gms protein (x 4 Calories/gm = 29.2 Calories)
  11.3 gms carbohydrate (x 4 Calories/gm = 45.2 Calories)
        7.3 gms protein (x 4 Calories/gm = 29.2 Calories)
                          TOTAL = 145.5 Calories

The number of Calories in a cup of whole milk can be calculated through simple multiplication and addition, as shown above.

Part A of this activity brings out the dual role of protein, emphasizing the primary role it plays in building body tissue. The story "The Do It

Activity

127

Yourselfers-Builders, Not Burners," implies that structural proteins in our bodies (muscles, collagen in bones) are broken down for energy if carbohydrates or fats fail to provide enough energy. This breaking down occurs only when food intake is very low. Young children in underdeveloped countries and in poverty pockets of developed countries are especially vulnerable.

Part B applies the Calorie value (per gram) of the three energy-yielding nutrients in determining the Calorie content of specific servings of food. Foods used are those containing all three energy-yielding nutrients. Prior to beginning with Part B, reproduce enough copies of the worksheet Food Labels with Energy-Yielding Nutrients so that when it is cut into individual labels, each student will have three labels. Cut out the labels and place them in a container.

Materials Needed
The Do-It-Yourselfers: Builders, Not Burners
Food Labels with Energy-Yielding Nutrients
one empty container (coffee can, shoe box, big envelope, etc.)

Part A
You will narrate the story about a family called the Do-It-Yourselfers. It should be used as an analogy to the role of the structural proteins in our body. Following the story, the questions pertaining to energy sources, structures, and concepts should be discussed.

The Do-It-Yourselfers: Builders, Not Burners

Everybody hopes to own a nice home someday. One particular family, called the Do-It-Yourselfers, decided to build their own home because it was too expensive to buy another family's house. They found an empty lot in town, big enough to build a lovely wooden home. The new Do-It-Yourselfers' house even had a wooden porch in the front for Ma and Pa Do-It-Yourselfer to sit in their rockers.

Winter was hard for the Do-It-Yourselfer family. They burned a lot of coal in their stove to keep warm. Once it snowed so hard it didn't stop for a whole week. The family ran out of coal; so they had to find another way to heat their home. Shivering from the cold, Pa Do-It-Yourselfer took his son out on the porch. And do you know what they did? They chopped up the porch into logs and burned them in their coal stove!

Pa Do-It-Yourselfer hated to chop up his lovely porch, but he had to keep his family warm. In the spring, Pa rebuilt the wooden porch. And if you walk by their home in the summer, you will see Ma and Pa Do-It-Yourselfer rocking away on the front porch.

1. Energy sources.
   a) What did the family in this story normally burn for fuel in their stove? (coal)
   b) What two nutrients do our bodies usually burn for energy? (fats and carbohydrates, rather than protein)
2. Structures.
   a) What is the family's home and porch made out of? (wood)
   b) What nutrient makes up a lot of our body tissue? (Protein. Hair, teeth, bones, skin, and organs within our body are *all* examples of body tissue made of protein.)

c) How is the wood in the family's home like protein in our body?
(Both are used for building structures, but they could be used for energy instead.)

3. Concepts
a) Why did the family have to burn wood from their porch for fuel?
(Because they ran out of coal.)
b) When do you think our bodies must use protein for energy?
(When there isn't enough energy from fats and carbohydrates to meet our energy needs.)
c) Are there any other situations in which our body would use protein for energy?
(Yes. Our body needs only a certain amount of protein for growth and repair of body tissue. When we eat more than that certain amount, the extra protein is burned as energy. Sometimes it is also changed to fat. Most Americans eat a lot of protein; usually there is extra left over to burn or store as fat.)

Part B

Referring back to Lesson 11, ask students to recollect the foods they used in loading the "energy input" side of the balance scale. Ask them how they suppose the energy (Caloric) values of the foods were determined, that is, what they would have to know about a food to determine the number of Calories it has. (The amount of fat, carbohydrate, and protein.) Explain to students that regardless of whether the body uses the protein in a food for tissue building or energy, the amount of protein in a food is always used to determine the food's Caloric value.

Illustrate the appropriate mathematical computation, using whole milk (refer to this lesson's Nutrition Information). Round off the nearest whole number if you don't want students working with decimals. Then have each student draw three of the food labels and make the appropriate calculations to determine the correct Caloric values. Students should:
1) Hand in their computations to be used as partial lesson evaluation, or
2) self-check their answers in a way designated by you.

Caloric values (rounded to the nearest whole number) of the foods:

Food	Serving Size	Calories
cheddar cheese	1¼ ounce	141
ice cream (vanilla)	½ cup	140
milk shake (chocolate)	1½ cup	405
bagel	1 medium	154
low-fat milk	1 cup	119
pancake	1 (4" diameter)	61
pizza	¼ of a 14" pizza	355
yogurt (flavored)	1 cup	225
chocolate milk	1 cup	221
peanut butter	2 tablespoons	200
peanuts	¼ cup	226
oatmeal	½ cup	67

__c__ 1. Susan needed 40 grams of protein each day for building and repairing body tissue. On one day she ate 60 grams of protein. What would happen to the extra 20 grams?
a. It would become a part of Susan's bones and teeth.
b. It would be excreted.

Evaluation

129

c. It would be used for energy or stored as fat.

d. It would be turned into vitamins.

_d_ 2. Sally, who was very thin, began swimming a mile each day. Sally's parents told her that she would have to eat extra Calories because of her exercise. However, Sally refused to do this. How would this affect the protein Sally ate?

a. More of the protein would be used to build her muscles.

b. Less of the protein would be used for energy.

c. More of the protein would be stored as fat.

d. More of the protein would be used for energy.

_d_ 3. Both carbohydrate and protein give four Calories per gram, but fat gives nine Calories per gram. A cup of eggnog has:

34 grams of carbohydrate

10 grams of protein

19 grams of fat

How many Calories are in one cup of eggnog?

a. 256 Calories

b. 152 Calories

c. 410 Calories

d. 347 Calories

_b_ 4. A cup of plain yogurt contains:

16 grams of carbohydrate

12 grams of protein

4 grams of fat

If carbohydrate and protein each supply four Calories per gram, and fat supplies nine Calories per gram, how many Calories are in the cup of yogurt?

a. 200 calories

b. 148 Calories

c. 108 Calories

d. 170 Calories

References and Resources

Books

Guthrie, H. A. 1979. *Introductory Nutrition.* 4th ed. St. Louis: The C.V. Mosby Co. $16.95 (T)

Films/Filmstrips

How a Hamburger Turns into You. 1978. Perennial Education Dept., 477 Roger Williams, P.O. Box 855, Ravinia Highland Park, IL 60035. Film, 16mm, color, sound, 19 minutes, study guide. $280/$28 rental. (S)

How Food Becomes You. 1964. National Dairy Council, 6300 N. River Road, Rosemont, IL 60018. Filmstrip, script, 15 minutes. $5 (S)

Articles

"Some Aspects of Protein Nutrition." 1972. *Dairy Council Digest* 43:6. (T)

Learning Packet

"Weight Reduction." 1978. Expanded Nutrition Program, 202 Wills House, Michigan State University, East Lansing, MI 48824. Workbook. $1.50 (S,T)

Food Labels with Energy-Yielding Nutrients

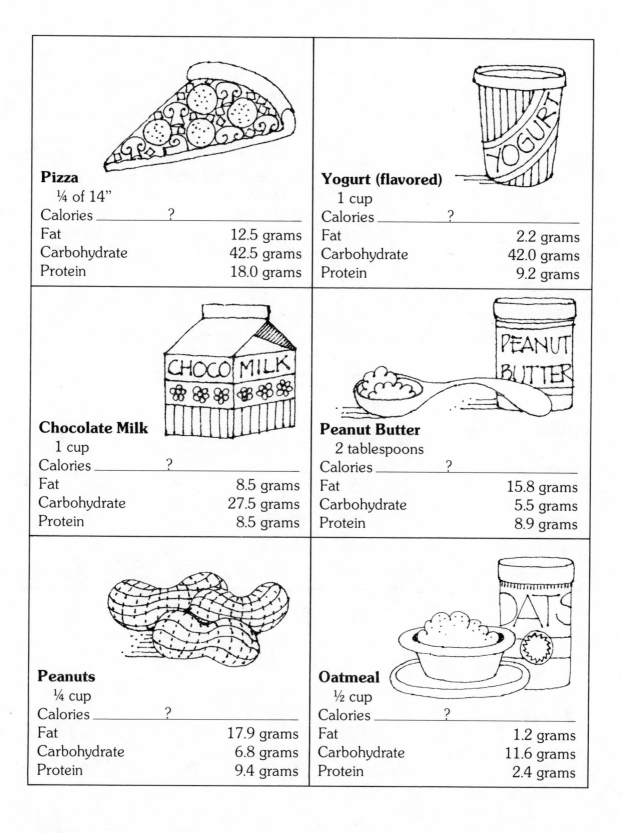

Pizza
¼ of 14"
Calories _____?_____
Fat   12.5 grams
Carbohydrate   42.5 grams
Protein   18.0 grams

Yogurt (flavored)
1 cup
Calories _____?_____
Fat   2.2 grams
Carbohydrate   42.0 grams
Protein   9.2 grams

Chocolate Milk
1 cup
Calories _____?_____
Fat   8.5 grams
Carbohydrate   27.5 grams
Protein   8.5 grams

Peanut Butter
2 tablespoons
Calories _____?_____
Fat   15.8 grams
Carbohydrate   5.5 grams
Protein   8.9 grams

Peanuts
¼ cup
Calories _____?_____
Fat   17.9 grams
Carbohydrate   6.8 grams
Protein   9.4 grams

Oatmeal
½ cup
Calories _____?_____
Fat   1.2 grams
Carbohydrate   11.6 grams
Protein   2.4 grams

Food Labels with Energy-Yielding Nutrients

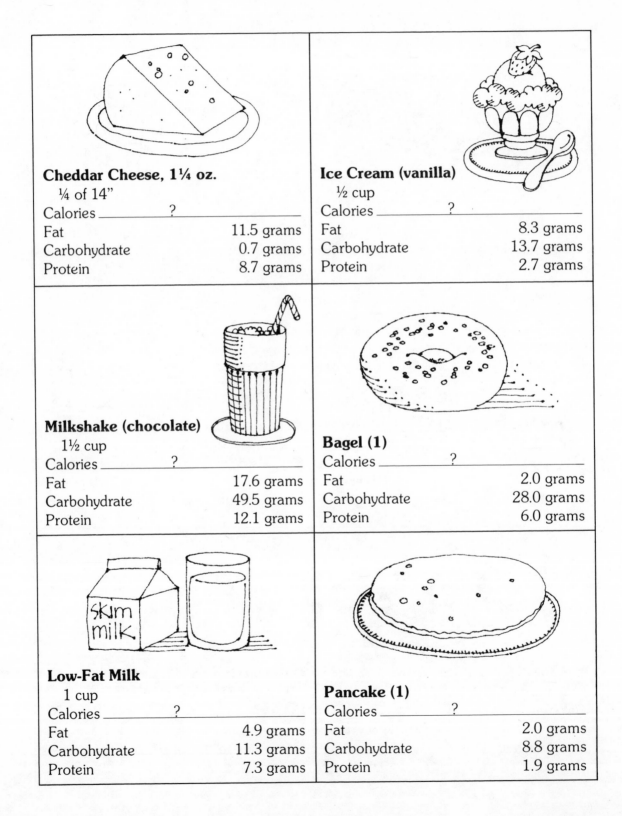

Cheddar Cheese, 1¼ oz.
   ¼ of 14"
Calories _____ ?
Fat   11.5 grams
Carbohydrate   0.7 grams
Protein   8.7 grams

Ice Cream (vanilla)
   ½ cup
Calories _____ ?
Fat   8.3 grams
Carbohydrate   13.7 grams
Protein   2.7 grams

Milkshake (chocolate)
   1½ cup
Calories _____ ?
Fat   17.6 grams
Carbohydrate   49.5 grams
Protein   12.1 grams

Bagel (1)
Calories _____ ?
Fat   2.0 grams
Carbohydrate   28.0 grams
Protein   6.0 grams

Low-Fat Milk
   1 cup
Calories _____ ?
Fat   4.9 grams
Carbohydrate   11.3 grams
Protein   7.3 grams

Pancake (1)
Calories _____ ?
Fat   2.0 grams
Carbohydrate   8.8 grams
Protein   1.9 grams

Lesson 21
It's a Small World

People from other cultures combine food in a variety of ways to obtain a balanced diet. Environment and cultural factors influence the preparation of the food.

While students help to prepare two food dishes from other cultures they should be able to 1) name two factors which will influence the preparation of a food; and 2) explain how cultural variations of a food contribute to a nutritious diet.

In this lesson the concept of variety in the diet is reemphasized as not only pleasurable but also the best way to insure an intake of the essential nutrients. Each culture influences the style of food preparation and to some extent the foods that are eaten. The environment of a culture also exerts a strong influence on a people's diet. The diet of a south seas island probably includes a wide variety of fruits, vegetables, and seafood. This is because of the tropical environment that favors the growth of many fruits and vegetables and because of the easy access to the sea for seafood. The diet of the island is characteristically low in grains because the weather conditions are not ideal for their growth.

  As you and the class prepare the foods in the activity, the following points should be stressed through questions and student answers.
● No single food supplies all the needed nutrients; therefore, only by combining ingredients can you get a balance of the nutrients you need.
● Balanced meals can be made by a variety of methods and with many different kinds of food.
● Trying new kinds of foods and experimenting with new ways to prepare it can be fun.

In this activity, students will learn that variations of a single food can be found in numerous cultures. Each country's adaptations of a food reflect its culture and environment, expressed in the spices and ingredients used, the mode of preparation, and the times when it is commonly served. An example of a food that recurs in several different cultural settings is the pancake. It is made with corn, flour, potatoes, rice, water, or milk. Eggs, leavening agents, and fat or oil may also be included. The

French refer to the pancake as a *crepe,* the Indians as a *chapathis,* and the Mexicans as a *tortilla.* Sometimes the tortillas are filled and rolled to make enchiladas or burritos. Almost every culture has a pancakelike dish. Consider, for example, eggrolls, manicotti, and dumplings. In this activity, choose two countries that vary in climate and customs, giving the students an opportunity to see how two very different groups of people utilize a similar food. A list of suggested countries and cultural foods follows.

Suggested Countries and Their Cultural Foods

Country	*Name of Food*
Mexico	Tortilla: unleavened bread usually made with cornmeal.
	Enchilada: tortilla filled (rolled) with cheese and/or meat and baked in a spicy tomato sauce.
India	Chapathis: unleavened bread, usually an accompaniment to curries and other vegetables.
France	Crepe: paper thin pancake filled with meat or fruit.
China (Peking)	Mu Shu Pork: thin pancake served with a combination of vegetables, eggs, and shredded pork.
China	Eggroll: thin pancake filled with a combination of vegetables and chicken, pork, or shrimp. It is rolled and deep-fat fried.
	Wonton: thin pancake similar to the one used for eggrolls, filled with meat and fried or used in soups.
Russia	Filled Dumplings
Poland	Nalesniki: a pancake that can be filled with meat, cheese, or mushroom combinations and served as an entrée. Those filled with sweet things and fried with butter are served as dessert.

The activity, depending on the depth of outside work, will take more than two class sessions to complete.

Materials Needed
Food Composition Table for Selected Nutrients (Appendix D)
A Nutrient Profile
library reference material
ingredients to make two cultural foods (as chosen by the two groups of students)

Part A
   Divide the class into Group A and Group B. Each group will focus on a country to study. Each student or a pair of students within each group will choose an aspect of the country and prepare a few short paragraphs after researching the topic. The reports could be combined to form a book on the country studied. Suggested areas to be researched are:

1. geography/weather
2. government
3. agriculture
4. history
5. clothing
6. architecture
7. art
8. education
9. music
10. animals
11. customs/holidays
12. religions

Part B

Each group should prepare a food from the country they present. All students should sample the different foods. Conduct a discussion relating the food to cultural and environmental factors, described in the group reports from Part A. The various adaptations of a simple food, such as a pancake, should be recognized as a method to increase variety in one's diet.

Several books containing recipes of pancakes or flat breads have been included in the References and Resources section. A list of foods and countries appropriate for this activity have been suggested.

Following the discussion and tasting session, each student should complete the worksheet A Nutrient Profile for each food. Total Calories and the percentage of the U.S. RDA for the Iron CaPAC nutrients for each cultural food should be presented to the class. Perhaps A Nutrient Profile for each food could be posted on the bulletin board.

Each student's written report combined with the worksheet A Nutrient Profile could serve as the evaluation for this lesson. Suggested quiz items are also given.

Evaluation

   <u>d</u> 1. The foods common to each culture are influenced by
      a. the climate
      b. the religious beliefs and customs
      c. the geography
      d. all of the above
   <u>b</u> 2. Foods should be served in a number of ways because
      a. it is necessary to hide certain food odors.
      b. it increases variety in the diet.
      c. it will improve the nutrient quality of the food.
      d. it will preserve the flavor of the food for longer periods of time.

Books

References and Resources

Helfman, E. S. 1970. *This Hungry World.* New York: Lothrop, Lee and Shephard Co. $6.48 (S)

Johnson, L. S. 1969. *What We Eat: The Origins and Travels of Foods around the World.* New York: Rand McNally and Co. $4.95 (S)

O'Connell, L.; Rye, J., and Bell, P. 1981. *Nutrition in a Changing World: A Curriculum for Grade Four.* Provo, Utah: Brigham Young University Press. (T)

Shapiro, R. 1972. *A Whole World of Cooking.* Boston: Little, Brown and Co. 1972. $5.95 (S)

Spieler, D., and Spieler, M. 1974. *Naturally Good, International Whole Food Recipes.* New York: Grove Press. $3.95 (T)

Films/Filmstrips

Chinese Food: Origins and Preparation. 1977. American Ethnic Foods, Butterick, 708 Third Avenue, New York 10017. Two filmstrips/ audiocassette/teaching packet, color. $80 plus 5% shipping and handling. (S,T)

German Food: Origins and Preparation. 1977. American Ethnic Foods, Butterick, 708 Third Avenue, New York 10017. Two filmstrips/ audiocassette/teaching packet, color. $80 plus 5% shipping and handling. (S,T)

Italian Food: Origins and Preparation. 1977. American Ethnic Foods, Butterick, 708 Third Avenue, New York 10017. Two filmstrips/ audiocassette/teaching packet, color. $80 plus 5% shipping and handling. (S,T)

The Big Dinner Table. 1978. Dairy Council of Alabama Inc., 9 Office Park, Birmingham, AL 35201. Film, color, 11 minutes. Free loan. (S)

A Nutrient Profile

Name_____

Food Prepared:_____

_____

Percentage of U.S. RDA

_____

Ingredient	*Amount*	*Calories*	*Iron*	*Protein*	*Vit A*	*Vit C*	*Calcium*

TOTAL_____

Glossary for Teachers

allowance: a provision or amount of something. In this lesson allowance refers to a regular amount of a nutrient.

amino acids: building blocks of proteins. Enzymes help break down protein into amino acids.

average: the arithmetic mean. This is found by adding a list of numbers that all relate to the same thing and dividing the total by the number of items in the list.

basal metabolism: those vital processes required to sustain life when the body is at complete rest. This includes synthesis of bones, teeth, muscle, hormones, enzymes, bile, and hemoglobin. Maintenance of body temperature, blood circulation, brain function, respiration, glandular activity, and muscle tonus are also included. Energy needs for basal metabolism are very high, averaging 1700 Calories per day for the average American male.

Calorie (kilocalorie or Kcal): a measure of heat energy. In nutrition, the kilocalorie is used to measure the energy value of food ingested and activity expended. Usually when we talk about kilocalories, we refer to them as "Calories."

carbohydrate: a nutrient in food made of carbon, hydrogen, and oxygen. Carbohydrates provide energy to the body. Sugars and starches are two common carbohydrates in foods.

carbon dioxide: a colorless, odorless, tasteless gas found in the atmosphere. People exhale it as a waste product that makes up a major part of their exhaled breath.

catalyst: a substance that accelerates a reaction. Enzymes work as catalysts.

citrus fruits: grapefruit, lemons, limes, and oranges—all of which supply vitamin C.

collagen: a protein network that forms various kinds of connecting tissue. For bone it is the network in which bone crystals form. Vitamin C and iron help collagen formation.

crystal: a solid having symmetrical surfaces. Common crystals are salt, sugar, and gems. In bone, the crystals are calcium phosphate, the formation of which is assisted by vitamin D.

dietary survey: a way of evaluating the diet of an individual or of a group to learn whether the diet is adequate or inadequate for the individual's or the group's needs.

digestion and absorption: processes that prepare ingested foods to enter the blood and cells. Energy for digestion and absorption is not included in energy for basal metabolism and is believed to be around 10 percent of the total energy needed.

enzymes: materials made by the body for increasing the speed of chemical reactions. Enzymes are composed of amino acids; they are a protein.

experiment: a test set up to solve a problem or answer a question.

fat: the substance stored in the body's fat cells. Fat is also one of the nutrients found in food. Both kinds of fats are made of carbon, hydrogen, and oxygen. Fat provides energy to the body. The body uses its fat stores to pad vital organs, insulate the body, act as a shock absorber, and provide energy.

fatty acids: building parts of fat. Enzymes help break down fats into fatty acids.

foundation: the base of a wall, house, or other structure. In bone, the foundation includes the collagen and ground substance, which together are called the "bone matrix."

glucose: a simple sugar made from the digestion of carbohydrates. Glucose is the sugar found in blood. Starch is composed of thousands of glucose molecules joined together.

glycerides: fats.

glycerol: a substance to which fatty acids are attached to form fat. Another name for fat is glyceride.

glycogen: the form in which animals store glucose—sometimes referred to as "animal starch." The human body can store only small amounts of glucose as glycogen. Once glycogen stores are full, any excess glucose is converted into fat and stored as fat tissue.

ground substance: the cementlike substance in which collagen fibers are embedded. It is mainly composed of protein and carbohydrates. Vitamin A helps ground substance formation.

hemoglobin: the substance in our blood that carries oxygen and gives blood its color. Hemoglobin is made by special cells in our body.

hydroxyapatite: crystals of bone mineral, mainly composed of calcium phosphate. It gives strength to the bone matrix.

internal: inside; for example, the liver is an internal organ because it is inside the body.

legumes: a category of foods belonging in the meat group of the basic four food groups; legumes include dry beans, peas, and peanuts.

matrix: framework of a tissue that includes cells and the materials they secrete.

minerals: the noncombustible fraction of food; ash inorganic substances. Examples are iron, calcium, and phosphorus.

minimum amount: the smallest quantity of a substance needed.

organ: a body part with one or more specific functions. Examples of organs are the heart, the skin, the brain, and the kidneys.

organic compound: any chemical compound containing carbon. Examples include carbohydrates, fats, proteins, and tissues from plants, people, and other animals.

phosphorus: a nonmetallic chemical element making up about one percent of the body weight. Most of the phosphorus in the body is found in hydroxyapatite crystals of teeth and bones. The rest is distributed throughout all the cells of the body. It plays an important role in many body processes. Phosphorus is especially important in reactions involving uptake or release of energy.

photosynthesis: the process through which plants use sunlight to change water and carbon dioxide into starch.

physical activity: physical movements by parts of the body that require energy. The amount of energy depends upon the type and duration of the activity and the body size of the person performing the activity.

population: in this curriculum, the whole set of people from which a sample is taken.

protein: a nutrient that contains a variety of amino acids having nitrogen as a basic part. Most often in our culture protein is equated with meat, poultry, dairy products, and seafood as primary sources, but legumes also contain substantial amounts of protein. Other cultures use mixtures of legumes and grains as their primary source of protein.

Recommended Dietary Allowance (RDA): a dietary guideline set by scientists after careful study. The RDA is the amount of an essential nutrient believed to be adequate to meet the needs of most healthy persons.

requirement: a need; a prerequisite condition; an essential element.

rickets: a disease resulting from a vitamin D deficiency, characterized by weak bone structure.

safety factor: a protective device. In this curriculum it is the amount of a nutrient added to the average requirement for that nutrient to yield a total large enough to keep most people from nutritional risk.

sample: a group of individuals representative of the whole population.

scurvy: a disease resulting from a vitamin C deficiency, characterized by weakness, sore joints, anemia, and spongy gums.

triglycerides: fats with three fatty acids attached to the glycerol.

vitamin D: a fat-soluble vitamin. The body is capable of producing vitamin D from a precursor in the skin in the presence of sunlight. It also obtains vitamin D in certain foods. Vitamin D promotes normal calcification of bone.

vitamins: nutrients that are found in minute quantities of food. Vitamins, unlike carbohydrates, proteins, and fats, are not sources of energy. Instead, vitamins function to help regulate body processes by aiding enzymes.

water: a nutrient made of hydrogen and oxygen (H_2O) that makes up between 60 and 70 percent of the body's total weight. Water is the main vehicle for transporting materials through the body. It also helps the body eliminate wastes.

Key Nutrients in Foods

Iron CaPAC Nutrients	Major Functions:	*Important Food Sources
Protein	Builds and repairs all body tissues; supplies energy	1. Lean meats, poultry, fish, seafoods, eggs, milk, cheeses, yogurt 2. Dry beans, peas, nuts, seeds 3. Cereals and breads
Calcium	Builds bones and teeth; helps nerves, muscles, and heart work properly; helps blood clot	1. Milk, cheeses and other milk products 2. Sardines, clams, oysters, canned salmon, dark green leafy vegetables
Iron	Helps build red blood cells; helps cells use oxygen	1. Liver, kidney, heart, and fortified breakfast cereals listing at least 45% U.S. RDA of iron per serving. 2. Oysters, lean red meat, prune juice and cooked dried beans 3. Whole grain and enriched bread and cereals, dried fruits, leafy greens, and egg yolks
Vitamin A	Helps eyes adjust to dim light; promotes healthy skin and lining tissues; helps the body resist infection; promotes growth	1. Liver 2. Deep yellow fruits and vegetables, dark green vegetables 3. Egg yolk, butter and fortified margarine
Vitamin C (ascorbic acid)	Helps tissues such as gums, blood vessels, bones, and teeth be healthy; promotes healing	1. Citrus fruits and juices, broccoli, strawberries, collards, mustard —greens, and turnip greens 2. Tomatoes, cantaloupe, spinach, and raw cabbage

*Foods listed after *1.* are the richest sources, after *2.* the second richest. For some nutrients the third richest sources are listed also (after *3.*).

Key Nutrients in Foods
According to Relative Cost

Iron CaPAC Nutrients	Less Expensive Food Sources:	More Expensive Food Sources:
Protein	Dried beans, peas, dried milk, peanut butter, chicken, pork liver, beef liver, fish, turkey, heart, kidney, eggs, ground beef, lentils, black-eyed peas, garbanzo beans	Steaks (rib, porterhouse, T-bone, sirloin), rib roast, fresh salmon, smoked oysters, lobster, lamb, veal sardines
Calcium	Milk (dried, skimmed, or canned), dark green leafy vegetables, homemade soy bean curd (tofu)	Fresh fluid milk, cheese, sardines, buttermilk
Iron	Pork or beef liver, kidney, heart, dried beans, dried peas, eggs, turnip and mustard greens, lima beans, soybeans, kidney beans, lentils, whole grain and enriched breads, and cereals	Steaks, calf liver, dried fruits, cashews
Vitamin A	Margarine, carrots, mustard or turnip greens, collards, kale, eggs, sweet potatoes, peppers, yams	Broccoli, asparagus, brussels sprouts, papaya, spinach greens, avocado
Vitamin C (ascorbic acid)	Cabbage, white potatoes cooked in skins, sweet potatoes (in season: cantaloupe, watermelon, strawberries, green and red peppers)	Fresh citrus fruits (out of season: green and red peppers, strawberries, cantaloupe, watermelon, broccoli, brussels sprouts, mango, cauliflower, papaya, nectarines, avocado)

The Basic Four Food Groups

From This Food Group	One Serving Equals	These People	Need This Number of Servings Each Day
Milk and Milk Products Major nutrients contributed: calcium and protein	1 cup fluid milk (whole, low fat, skimmed, buttermilk, reconstituted nonfat dried milk or evaporated milk) 1 cup yogurt 1 ounce hard cheese ½ cup cottage cheese ½ to ⅔ cup ice cream A cup of fluid milk or yogurt provide the most calcium. To get as much calcium from the other three foods, you would need 1½ oz. of hard cheese, 1½ cups of cottage cheese or 2 cups of ice cream.	Children under 9 years old Children 9 to 12 years Teenagers Adults Pregnant women	2 to 3 3 or more 4 or more 2 or more 4 or more

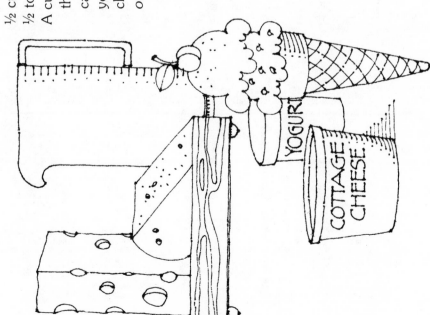

The Basic Four Food Groups

From This Food Group	One Serving Equals	These People	Need This Number of Servings Each Day
Meat and Meat Alternates Major nutrients contributed: protein and iron	2 ounces lean, cooked meat or poultry (without bone) 2 ounces cooked fish or shellfish 1 cup cooked dried beans, peas, or lentils 2 eggs ⅓ to ½ cup nuts or seeds 4 tablespoons peanut butter *½ cup cottage cheese *2 ounces hard cheese *These two foods may also count toward milk-group servings. All of the foods above, in the amounts given, provide about the same amount of protein.	All ages Pregnant women	2 or more 3 or more

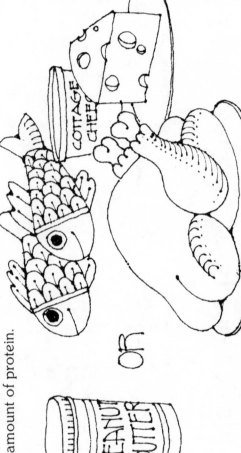

The Basic Four Food Groups

From This Food Group	One Serving Equals	These People	Need This Number of Servings Each Day
Breads and Cereals Major nutrients contributed: Iron	1 slice bread / 1 roll or muffin ½ hamburger bun ½ cup cooked cereal, rice, macaroni, noodles, etc. 1 ounce (usually ¾ to 1 cup ready-to-eat cereal 4 to 5 crackers (2 inches square)	All ages	4 or more

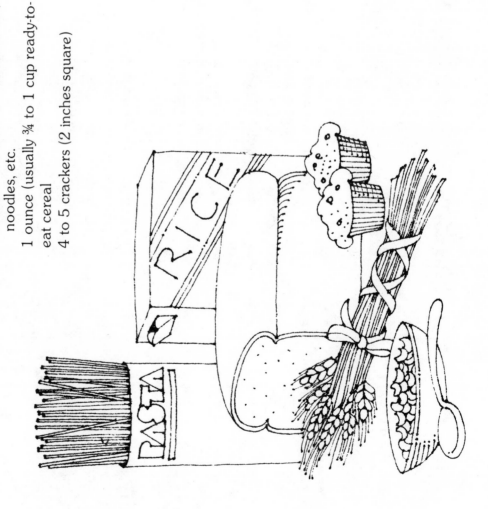

The Basic Four Food Groups

From This Food Group	One Serving Equals	These People	Need This Number of Servings Each Day
Fruits and Vegetables Major nutrients contributed:	½ cup if cooked or a juice ⅔ to 1 cup if raw and cut into pieces	All ages	a total or 4 or more as follows:
vitamin C from citrus fruits, citrus juices, and certain other fruits and vegetables	1 medium, if commonly eaten whole Grapefruit, orange, lemon, lime, strawberries, cantaloupe, tomato, or green or red pepper, and broccoli.		one C each day
vitamin A from dark green and bright yellow fruits and vegetables	Apricots, carrots, okra, chard, mustard greens, spinach, winter squash, turnip greens, sweet potatoes, string beans, collards, or broccoli.		one A at least every other day
	Apples, bananas, beets, cauliflower, celery, onions, corn, cucumbers, dates, eggplant, parsnips, peaches, pears, plums, potatoes, prunes, rhubarb, summer squash, cherries, berries, artichokes, or rutabaga.		2 or 3 others each day

The Basic Four Food Groups

From This Food Group	One Serving Equals	These People	Need This Number of Servings Each Day
Additional Foods Major nutrients contributed: These foods contribute calories but are poor sources of Protein, Vitamins and Minerals.	Varying amounts of Fats, oils, salad dressings, and butter; sugars, honey, syrups, jam, jelly and candy; most pastries, cakes and pies; soda pop; condiments, such as mustard and catsup.	All ages	*No recommended number of servings. Most of the daily calories should come from the basic four food groups. Therefore, only small amounts of these foods should be eaten.*

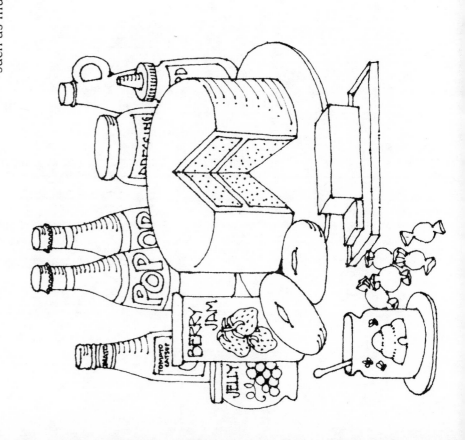

The following tables have been reproduced from the text, *RDA, Ninth Edition 1980*, by the National Academy of Sciences. They include tables on (a) Recommended Dietary Allowances for protein, fat-soluble vitamins, and water-soluble vitamins, and minerals; (b)

estimates of adequate and safe intakes of selected vitamins, trace elements, and electrolytes; and (c) recommended energy intakes, together with mean heights and weights.

FOOD AND NUTRITION BOARD, NATIONAL ACADEMY OF SCIENCES–NATIONAL RESEARCH COUNCIL

Recommended Daily Dietary Allowances[a]

Revised 1980

Designed for the maintenance of good nutrition of practically all healthy people in the U.S.A.

	Age (years)	Weight (kg)	Weight (lb)	Height (cm)	Height (in)	Protein (g)	Vitamin A (µg RE)[b]	Vitamin D (µg)[c]	Vitamin E (mg α-TE)[d]	Vitamin C (mg)	Thiamin (mg)	Riboflavin (mg)	Niacin (mg NE)[e]	Vitamin B-6 (mg)	Folacin (µg)[f]	Vitamin B-12 (µg)	Calcium (mg)	Phosphorus (mg)	Magnesium (mg)	Iron (mg)	Zinc (mg)	Iodine (µg)
Infants	0.0–0.5	6	13	60	24	kg×2.2	420	10	3	35	0.3	0.4	6	0.3	30	0.5[g]	360	240	50	10	3	40
	0.5–1.0	9	20	71	28	kg×2.0	400	10	4	35	0.5	0.6	8	0.6	45	1.5	540	360	70	15	5	50
Children	1–3	13	29	90	35	23	400	10	5	45	0.7	0.8	9	0.9	100	2.0	800	800	150	15	10	70
	4–6	20	44	112	44	30	500	10	6	45	0.9	1.0	11	1.3	200	2.5	800	800	200	10	10	90
	7–10	28	62	132	52	34	700	10	7	45	1.2	1.4	16	1.6	300	3.0	800	800	250	10	10	120
Males	11–14	45	99	157	62	45	1000	10	8	50	1.4	1.6	18	1.8	400	3.0	1200	1200	350	18	15	150
	15–18	66	145	176	69	56	1000	10	10	60	1.4	1.7	18	2.0	400	3.0	1200	1200	400	18	15	150
	19–22	70	154	177	70	56	1000	7.5	10	60	1.5	1.7	19	2.2	400	3.0	800	800	350	10	15	150
	23–50	70	154	178	70	56	1000	5	10	60	1.4	1.6	18	2.2	400	3.0	800	800	350	10	15	150
	51+	70	154	178	70	56	1000	5	10	60	1.2	1.4	16	2.2	400	3.0	800	800	350	10	15	150
Females	11–14	46	101	157	62	46	800	10	8	50	1.1	1.3	15	1.8	400	3.0	1200	1200	300	18	15	150
	15–18	55	120	163	64	46	800	10	8	60	1.1	1.3	14	2.0	400	3.0	1200	1200	300	18	15	150
	19–22	55	120	163	64	44	800	7.5	8	60	1.1	1.3	14	2.0	400	3.0	800	800	300	18	15	150
	23–50	55	120	163	64	44	800	5	8	60	1.0	1.2	13	2.0	400	3.0	800	800	300	18	15	150
	51+	55	120	163	64	44	800	5	8	60	1.0	1.2	13	2.0	400	3.0	800	800	300	10	15	150
Pregnant						+30	+200	+5	+2	+20	+0.4	+0.3	+2	+0.6	+400	+1.0	+400	+400	+150	h	+5	+25
Lactating						+20	+400	+5	+3	+40	+0.5	+0.5	+5	+0.5	+100	+1.0	+400	+400	+150	h	+10	+50

Fat-Soluble Vitamins	Water-Soluble Vitamins	Minerals

[a] The allowances are intended to provide for individual variations among most normal persons as they live in the United States under usual environmental stresses. Diets should be based on a variety of common foods in order to provide other nutrients for which human requirements have been less well defined. See text for detailed discussion of allowances and of nutrients not tabulated. See Table 1 (p. 20) for weights and heights by individual year of age. See Table 3 (p. 23) for suggested average energy intakes.

[b] Retinol equivalents. 1 retinol equivalent = 1 µg retinol or 6 µg β carotene. See text for calculation of vitamin A activity of diets as retinol equivalents.

[c] As cholecalciferol. 10 µg cholecalciferol = 400 IU of vitamin D.

[d] α-tocopherol equivalents. 1 mg d-α tocopherol = 1 α-TE. See text for variation in allowances and calculation of vitamin E activity of the diet as α-tocopherol equivalents.

[e] 1 NE (niacin equivalent) is equal to 1 mg of niacin or 60 mg of dietary tryptophan.

[f] The folacin allowances refer to dietary sources as determined by *Lactobacillus casei* assay after treatment with enzymes (conjugases) to make polyglutamyl forms of the vitamin available to the test organism.

[g] The recommended dietary allowance for vitamin B-12 in infants is based on average concentration of the vitamin in human milk. The allowances after weaning are based on energy intake (as recommended by the American Academy of Pediatrics) and consideration of other factors, such as intestinal absorption; see text.

[h] The increased requirement during pregnancy cannot be met by the iron content of habitual American diets nor by the existing iron stores of many women; therefore the use of 30–60 mg of supplemental iron is recommended. Iron needs during lactation are not substantially different from those of nonpregnant women, but continued supplementation of the mother for 2–3 months after parturition is advisable in order to replenish stores depleted by pregnancy.

Estimated Safe and Adequate Daily Dietary Intakes of Selected Vitamins and Minerals[a]

Vitamins

	Age (years)	Vitamin K (µg)	Biotin (µg)	Pantothenic Acid (mg)
Infants	0–0.5	12	35	2
	0.5–1	10–20	50	3
Children	1–3	15–30	65	3
and	4–6	20–40	85	3–4
Adolescents	7–10	30–60	120	4–5
	11+	50–100	100–200	4–7
Adults		70–140	100–200	4–7

Trace Elements[b]

	Age (years)	Copper (mg)	Manganese (mg)	Fluoride (mg)	Chromium (mg)	Selenium (mg)	Molybdenum (mg)
Infants	0–0.5	0.5–0.7	0.5–0.7	0.1–0.5	0.01–0.04	0.01–0.04	0.03–0.06
	0.5–1	0.7–1.0	0.7–1.0	0.2–1.0	0.02–0.06	0.02–0.06	0.04–0.08
Children	1–3	1.0–1.5	1.0–1.5	0.5–1.5	0.02–0.08	0.02–0.08	0.05–0.1
and	4–6	1.5–2.0	1.5–2.0	1.0–2.5	0.03–0.12	0.03–10.12	0.06–0.15
Adoles-	7–10	2.0–2.5	2.0–3.0	1.5–2.5	0.05–0.2	0.05–0.2	0.10–0.3
cents	11+	2.0–3.0	2.5–5.0	1.5–2.5	0.05–0.2	0.05–0.2	0.15–0.5
Adults		2.0–3.0	2.5–5.0	1.5–4.0	0.05–0.2	0.05–0.2	0.15–0.5

Electrolytes

	Age (years)	Sodium (mg)	Potassium (mg)	Chloride (mg)
Infants	0–0.5	115–350	350–925	275–700
	0.5–1	250–750	425–1275	400–1200
Children	1–3	325–975	550–1650	500–1500
and	4–6	450–1350	775–2325	700–2100
Adolescents	7–10	600–1800	1000–3000	925–2775
	11+	900–2700	1525–4575	1400–4200
Adults		1100–3300	1875–5625	1700–5100

[a]Because there is less information on which to base allowances, these figures are not given in the main table of RDA and are provided here in the form of ranges of recommended intakes.

[b]Since the toxic levels for many trace elements may be only several times usual intakes, the upper levels for the trace elements given in this table should not be habitually exceeded.

Mean Heights and Weights
and Recommended Energy Intake[a]

Category	Age (years)	Weight (kg)	Weight (lb)	Height (cm)	Height (in.)	Energy Needs (with range) (kcal)		(MJ)
Infants	0.0–0.5	6	13	60	24	kg x 115	(95–145)	kg x 0.48
	0.5–1.0	9	20	71	28	kg x 105	(80–135)	kg x 0.44
Children	1–3	13	29	90	35	1300	(900–1800)	5.5
	4–6	20	44	112	44	1700	(1300–2300)	7.1
	7–10	28	62	132	52	2400	(1650–3300)	10.1
Males	11–14	45	99	157	62	2700	(2000–3700)	11.3
	15–18	66	145	176	69	2800	(2100–3900)	11.8
	19–22	70	154	177	70	2900	(2500–3300)	12.2
	23–50	70	154	178	70	2700	(2300–3100)	11.3
	51–75	70	154	178	70	2400	(2000–2800)	10.1
	76+	70	154	178	70	2050	(1650–2450)	8.6
Females	11–14	46	101	157	62	2200	(1500–3000)	9.2
	15–18	55	120	163	64	2100	(1200–3000)	8.8
	19–22	55	120	163	64	2100	(1700–2500)	8.8
	23–50	55	120	163	64	2000	(1600–2400)	8.4
	51–75	55	120	163	64	1800	(1400–2200)	7.6
	76+	55	120	163	64	1600	(1200–2000)	6.7
Pregnancy						+300		
Lactation						+500		

[a]The data in this table have been assembled from the observed median heights and weights of children shown in Table 1, together with desirable weights for adults given in Table 2 for the mean heights of men (70 in.) and women (64 in.) between the ages of 18 and 34 years as surveyed in the U.S. population (HEW/NCHS data).

The energy allowances for the young adults are for men and women doing light work. The allowances for the two older age groups represent mean energy needs over these age spans, allowing for a 2-percent decrease in basal (resting) metabolic rate per decade and a reduction in activity of 200 kcal/day for men and women between 51 and 75 years, 500 kcal for men over 75 years, and 400 kcal for women over 75 years (see text). The customary range of daily energy output is shown in parentheses for adults and is based on a variation in energy needs of ±400 kcal at any one age (see text and Garrow, 1978), emphasizing the wide range of energy intakes appropriate for any group of people.

Energy allowances for children through age 18 are based on median energy intakes of children of these ages followed in longitudinal growth studies. The values in parentheses are 10th and 90th percentiles of energy intake, to indicate the range of energy consumption among children of these ages (see text).

Food Composition Table for Selected Nutrients

Food	Amount	Wt. Grams	Food energy Calories	Protein	Vitamin A	Vitamin C	Thiamin	Riboflavin	Niacin	Calcium	Iron
							Percentages of U.S. RDA				
Almonds, in shell	10	25	60	4	*	*	2	6	2	2	2
Apple, fresh (3/lb.)	1	150	80	*	2	10	2	2	*	*	2
dried, cooked, unsweetened	1 cup	255	200	2	*	*	2	4	2	2	2
Apple pie, 2-crust	1 slice	158	400	6	*	4	2	2	4	2	2
Applesauce, sweetened	1 cup	255	230	*	2	4	4	2	*	*	8
Apricots, fresh w/skin	3	114	60	2	60	20	2	2	4	2	2
dried, uncooked	10 med. halves	35	90	2	80	6	*	4	6	2	10
Asparagus, cooked	4 spears	60	10	2	10	25	6	6	4	2	2
Avocado, California	½ w/skin	120	190	4	6	25	8	15	8	2	4
Bacon	2 slices	15	90	10	*	*	6	2	4	*	2
Bagel, egg, 3" diam.	1	55	165	10	*	*	10	6	6	*	6
Banana, med.	1	175	100	2	4	20	4	4	4	*	4
Beans, dried, cooked (Great Northern)	1 cup	180	210	30	*	*	15	8	6	8	25
Bean sprouts, raw, Mung	1 cup	125	35	6	*	15	8	8	4	2	6
Bean sprouts, cooked, Mung	1 cup	105	35	6	*	35	10	8	4	2	8
Beet greens, cooked	1 cup	145	25	4	150	35	6	15	2	15	15
Beets, whole, fresh cooked	2	100	30	2	*	10	2	2	2	2	2
Biscuit, 2" diam.	1	28	100	4	*	*	6	4	4	4	8
Blueberries, raw	1 cup	145	90	2	2	35	2	6	4	2	8
Bologna	1 slice	28	80	8	*	*	4	4	4	*	2
Bouillon, beef	1 cup 240 ml	240	30	8	*	*	*	2	6	*	2

Food	Amount	Wt. Grams	Food energy Calories	Protein	Vitamin A	Vitamin C	Thiamin	Riboflavin	Niacin	Calcium	Iron
							Percentages of U.S. RDA				
Bread, enriched											
Cracked wheat	1 slice	25	70	4	*	*	2	2	2	2	2
Italian	1 slice	30	80	4	*	*	8	4	6	*	4
Rye (light)	1 slice	25	60	4	*	*	4	2	2	2	2
White, soft crumb	1 slice	25	70	4	*	*	6	4	4	2	4
Whole wheat, soft crumb	1 slice	28	70	4	*	*	6	2	4	2	4
Broccoli, cooked	1 cup	155	40	8	80	230	10	20	6	15	6
Brown sugar	1 cup	220	820	*	*	*	2	4	2	20	40
Butter	1 pat	5	35	*	4	*	*	*	*	*	*
Cabbage, cooked	1 cup	145	30	2	4	80	4	4	2	6	2
Cake											
plain/without icing	1 piece	86	310	6	2	*	2	4	*	6	2
with chocolate icing	1 piece	123	450	8	4	*	2	6	*	8	4
Devils food with chocolate icing	1 piece	69	230	4	2	*	2	4	*	4	4
Candy											
caramels, plain or chocolate	1 oz.	28	110	2	*	*	*	2	*	4	2
chocolate, milk	1 oz.	28	150	4	2	*	2	6	*	6	2
gumdrops, starch jelly pieces	1 oz.	28	100	*	*	*	*	*	*	*	*
hard	1 oz.	28	110	*	*	*	*	*	*	*	2
peanut bars	1 oz.	28	140	8	*	*	8	2	15	2	2
peanut brittle	1 oz.	28	120	2	*	*	2	*	4	*	4
Cantaloupe	½ melon	477	80	2	180	150	8	4	8	4	6
Carrots, raw	6 to 8 strips, 1 oz.	28	10	*	60	4	2	*	*	2	2
Cauliflower, cooked	1 cup	125	30	4	2	120	8	6	4	2	4
Celery	1 stalk	40	8	*	2	6	*	*	*	2	*
Cereal, ready-to-eat, enriched**	1 oz.	28	110	4	20	20	25	25	20	*	20
Cheese											
American, pasteurized processed	1 slice	28	110	15	6	*	*	8	*	20	2

Food	Amount	Wt. (Grams)	Food energy (Calories)	Protein	Vitamin A	Vitamin C	Thiamin	Riboflavin	Niacin	Calcium	Iron
							Percentages of U.S. RDA				
Parmesan, grated	1 oz.	28	130	25	8	*	*	15	*	40	*
Chef salad ingredients:											
tomato, raw	1	200	40	4	35	70	8	4	6	2	4
lettuce, chopped	1 cup	55	8	*	4	4	2	2	*	2	2
ham, lean only	3 oz.	85	180	60	*	*	35	15	25	2	20
cheese, Swiss	1 oz.	28	110	15	6	*	*	6	*	25	2
Total		368	338	79	45	74	45	27	31	31	28
Chicken, flesh only, broiled	3 oz.	85	120	45	2	*	2	10	40	*	8
Chili con carne	1 cup 240 ml	255	340	40	4	*	6	10	15	8	25
Chocolate chip cookies, commercial type	4	42	200	4	*	*	2	2	*	2	4
Cocoa, instant mix		28	100	8	*	2	2	10	*	15	2
Corn, canned	1 cup	165	130	6	10	10	4	4	8	*	4
Corn bread	1 piece	55	180	6	2	*	6	6	4	15	4
Corn grits, enriched	1 cup	245	130	4	240	*	6	4	4	*	4
Crackers, animal	5	13	60	2	*	*	*	*	*	*	*
butter, round	4	13	60	2	*	*	*	*	*	2	*
saltine	4	11	50	2	*	*	*	*	*	*	*
Cupcake, w/icing	1	48	170	4	2	*	2	2	*	6	2
without icing	1	33	120	2	*	*	*	2	*	6	2
Doughnut, cake	1	42	160	2	*	*	6	6	4	2	8
Egg, plain	1	50	80	15	10	*	2	8	*	2	6
scrambled, w/ milk and table fat	1	64	110	15	15	*	4	10	*	6	6
Float, ice cream	1	281	165	4	3	*	*	4	*	5	*
Flounder, baked	3 oz.	85	170	60	*	4	4	4	10	2	6
Fruit cocktail, heavy syrup	1 cup	255	190	2	8	8	4	2	4	2	6
Gelatin (Jello), plain	1 cup	240	140	6	*	*	*	*	*	*	*
Gingerbread, mix	1 piece	63	170	4	*	*	2	4	2	6	6
Graham crackers	2	14	60	2	*	*	*	2	*	*	2
Grape juice, frozen, concentrate	240 ml 1 cup	250	130	*	*	15	4	4	2	*	2
Grape juice drink, canned	240 ml 1 cup	250	140	*	*	70	2	2	2	*	2

Food	Amount	Wt. Grams	Food energy Calories	Protein	Vitamin A	Vitamin C	Thiamin	Riboflavin	Niacin	Calcium	Iron
							Percentages of U.S. RDA				
Grapefruit, pink	½	241	50	*	10	70	4	2	*	2	2
Grapefruit, white	½	241	45	*	*	70	4	2	*	2	2
Grapefruit juice, frozen concentrated, sweetened	240 ml 1 cup	248	120	2	*	140	4	2	2	2	4
Grapes, fresh	1 cup	160	110	2	4	10	6	2	2	2	4
Hamburger, no roll	3 oz.	85	270	50	*	*	4	10	25	*	15
Hoagie, 11"		516	918	70	51	74	26	36	20	50	18
Hot dog, no roll		56	170	15	*	*	6	6	6	*	4
Ice cream, regular	240 ml 1 cup	133	260	15	10	2	4	15	*	20	*
Jams and preserves	1 Tbs.	20	60	*	*	*	*	*	*	*	2
Lamb chop, loin, lean and fat	3.5 oz.	99	360	50	*	*	8	8	15	*	6
Lemonade, frozen, concentrated	240 ml, 1 cup	248	110	*	*	30	*	2	*	*	*
Lettuce, iceberg		55	8	*	4	4	2	2	*	2	2
Liver, beef, fried	3 oz.	85	200	50	910	40	15	210	70	*	40
Macaroni, cooked, hot	1 cup	140	160	8	*	*	15	6	8	2	8
Macaroni and cheese, canned	1 cup	240	230	20	6	*	8	15	4	20	6
Maple syrup	1 Tbs.	20	50	*	*	*	2	*	*	2	2
Margarine	1 pat	5	35	*	4	*	*	*	*	*	*
Marshmallows, plain	1 oz.	28	90	*	*	*	*	*	*	*	2
Milk drink, choc. (skim milk)	1 cup	250	190	20	4	4	6	25	2	25	2
Milk, fluid evaporated, unsweetened, undiluted	240 ml 1 cup	252	350	40	15	4	6	50	2	60	2
nonfat dry	240 ml 1 cup	242	80	20	10***	4	6	25	*	30	*
skim	240 ml 1 cup	245	90	20	10***	4	6	25	*	30	*
two percent	240 ml 1 cup	246	150	25	10***	4	6	30	*	35	*
whole	240 ml 1 cup	244	160	20	6	4	4	25	*	30	*

Food	Amount	Wt. Grams	Food energy Calories	Protein	Vitamin A	Vitamin C	Thiamin	Riboflavin	Niacin	Calcium	Iron
						Percentages of U.S. RDA					
Noodles, enriched	240 ml 1 cup	160	200	10	2	*	15	8	10	2	8
Oatmeal	240 ml 1 cup	240	130	8	*	*	15	2	*	2	8
Ocean perch, frozen, breaded, fried	3 oz.	88	280	35	*	*	6	6	8	2	6
Onions, raw, sliced	240 ml 1 cup	115	45	2	*	20	2	2	*	4	4
Orange, fresh	1	180	60	2	6	110	8	2	2	6	2
juice, concentrated	240 ml 1 cup	249	120	2	10	200	15	2	4	2	2
Pancakes, plain	1 cake	27	60	2	2	*	4	4	2	6	4
Peach, fresh	1	115	40	*	25	10	2	2	4	*	2
water packed, canned	1 cup	244	80	2	20	10	2	4	8	*	4
Peanut butter	1 Tbs.	16	90	8	*	*	2	2	10	*	2
Peanuts, roasted in shell	10 jumbo	27	110	10	*	*	4	2	15	2	2
Peanuts, salted	1 cup	144	810	80	*	*	30	10	120	10	15
Pear, fresh	1	180	100	2	*	10	2	4	*	2	2
Peas, cooked, fresh	1 cup	160	110	15	15	60	30	10	20	4	15
cooked, frozen	1 cup	160	110	10	20	35	30	8	15	3	15
canned	1 cup	170	150	10	25	25	10	6	6	4	20
Peppers (green)	1	90	16	2	6	160	4	4	2	*	2
Pineapple, fresh	1 cup	155	80	*	2	45	10	2	2	2	4
water packed, canned	1 cup	246	100	2	2	30	15	2	2	2	4
Pizza with cheese topping	1 piece	65	150	15	8	8	2	8	4	15	4
Plum, fresh	1	70	30	*	4	6	2	2	2	*	2
Popcorn, oil, and salt	1 cup	9	40	2	*	*	2	*	*	*	2
Potato baked, in skin	1	202	150	6	*	50	10	4	15	2	6
french fried, frozen	10 pieces	50	110	2	*	20	4	*	6	*	4
Potato chips	10 chips	20	110	2	*	4	2	*	4	*	2
Pork chop, broiled	2.7 oz.	78	310	45	*	*	50	15	25	*	15
Pretzel, thin	1	6	25	*	*	*	*	*	*	*	*
Prune, dried, uncooked	10	75	160	2	20	4	4	6	4	4	15

Food	Amount	Wt. Grams	Food energy Calories	Protein	Vitamin A	Vitamin C	Thiamin	Riboflavin	Niacin	Calcium	Iron
							Percentages of U.S. RDA				
Prune juice	240 ml 1 cup	256	200	2	30	8	2	2	4	4	60
Pudding, made w/ milk w/out cooking	1 cup	260	330	15	6	*	6	25	2	35	8
Pumpkin pie	1 piece	152	320	10	80	*	4	8	4	8	4
Pumpkin seeds, hulled	1 cup	140	770	90	2	*	25	15	15	8	90
Raisins	1½ oz.	43	120	2	*	*	4	2	*	2	8
Rice, enriched, hot	1 cup	205	220	6	*	*	15	2	10	2	10
Roast beef, sliced lean and fat	3 oz.	85	300	45	*	*	4	8	20	*	15
Roll, hamburger	1	40	120	6	*	*	10	6	6	2	5
hard	1	50	160	8	*	*	15	8	8	2	8
Salad oil	240 ml 1 cup	218	1930	*	*	*	*	*	*	*	*
Sodas cola type	240 ml 1 cup	247	90	*	*	*	*	*	*	*	*
cream	240 ml 1 cup	247	105	*	*	*	*	*	*	*	*
fruit flavored	240 ml 1 cup	248	110	*	*	*	*	*	*	*	*
Root beer	240 ml 1 cup	247	100	*	*	*	*	*	*	*	*
Soup, canned chicken noodle	240 ml 1 cup	240	60	6	*	*	2	2	4	*	2
cream of chicken	240 ml 1 cup	240	90	4	8	*	2	2	2	2	2
vegetarian veg.	240 ml 1 cup	245	80	4	60	*	4	2	4	2	6
Soup, dehydrated, made with water beef noodle	240 ml 1 cup	240	70	4	*	*	6	2	4	*	2
chicken noodle	240 ml 1 cup	240	60	2	*	*	4	2	2	*	2
tomato vegetable with noodles	240 ml 1 cup	240	70	2	10	8	4	2	2	*	2
Spaghetti with meat sauce	240 ml 1 cup	250	330	40	30	35	15	20	20	10	20

Food	Amount	Wt. Grams	Food energy Calories	Protein	Vitamin A	Vitamin C	Thiamin	Riboflavin	Niacin	Calcium	Iron
						Percentages of U.S. RDA					
Spareribs	3 oz.	85	370	40	*	*	25	10	15	*	10
Spinach, cooked	1 cup	180	40	8	290	80	8	15	4	15	20
Steak, sirloin, lean and fat	3 oz.	85	330	45	*	*	4	8	20	*	15
Strawberries, raw	1 cup	149	60	2	2	150	2	6	4	4	8
Sunflower seeds	1 cup	145	810	80	2	*	190	20	40	15	60
Sweet potato, baked in skin	1	146	160	4	180	40	6	4	4	4	6
Tangerine, med.	1	116	40	2	8	45	4	2	*	4	2
Tapioca pudding	1 cup	165	220	20	10	4	4	20	*	15	4
Tomato, canned, solid and liquid	1 cup	241	50	4	45	70	8	4	8	2	6
juice	240 ml 1 cup	243	45	4	40	70	8	4	10	2	10
fresh	1	200	40	4	35	70	8	4	6	2	4
Tomato catsup	1 Tbs.	15	16	*	4	4	*	*	*	*	*
Tuna, canned in oil	3 oz.	85	170	60	2	*	2	6	50	*	8
Tuna, canned in water	3 oz.	85	110	50	*	*	*	6	60	*	8
Turkey, light meat, no skin	3 oz.	85	150	60	2	*	2	8	45	*	6
Turnips	1 cup	155	35	2	*	60	4	4	2	6	4
Veal roast	3 oz.	85	230	50	*	*	8	15	35	*	15
Watermelon	1 wedge	926	110	4	50	50	8	8	4	2	10
Yogurt, skimmed milk	1 cup	245	120	20	4	4	6	25	*	30	*
whole milk	1 cup	245	150	15	6	4	4	25	*	25	*

*None or less than 1 percent.

**Based on average values; for more precise information refer to package label of specific cereal.

***Fortified with vitamin A.

HUMAN ENERGY UNIT MODEL

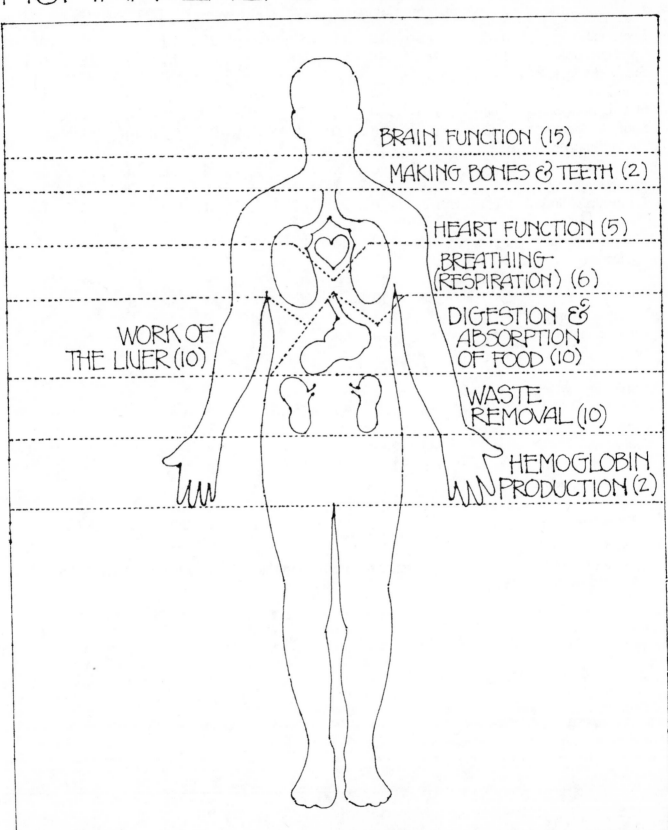

BRAIN FUNCTION (15)

MAKING BONES & TEETH (2)

HEART FUNCTION (5)

BREATHING (RESPIRATION) (6)

DIGESTION & ABSORPTION OF FOOD (10)

WASTE REMOVAL (10)

HEMOGLOBIN PRODUCTION (2)

WORK OF THE LIVER (10)

THE DIGESTIVE SYSTEM

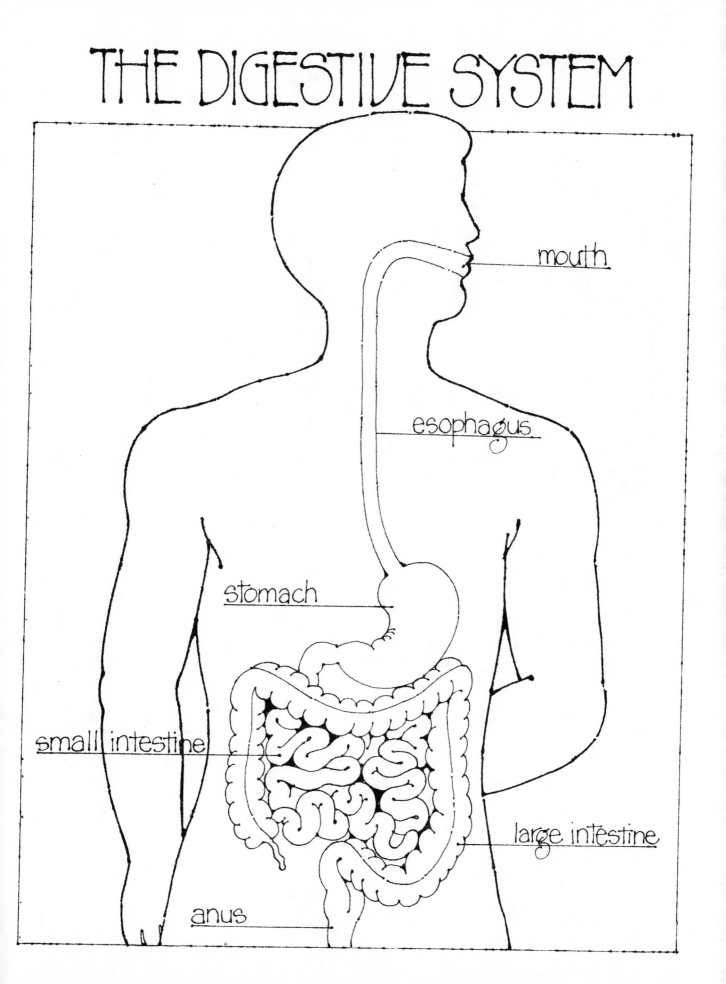

mouth

esophagus

stomach

small intestine

large intestine

anus

Appendix F

Fats in Foods

Food	Amount	Total Fat (grams)
bacon	2 strips	8.1
broccoli	½ cup	0.2
butter	2 pats	8.2
whole milk American cheese	1 slice	9.1
chocolate bar	1¾ ounces	8.9
coconut, shredded	2 T.	4.5
corn	½ cup	0.6
corn oil	1 T.	14.0
cottage cheese	½ cup	4.8
egg	1 large	5.7
hamburger, broiled	¼ lb.	23.0
hot dog	1	16.0
mayonnaise	1 T.	11.2
orange	large	0.5
peanut butter	1 T.	8.0
potato chips	12	11.0
rice, white	½ cup	0.1
skimmed milk	1 cup	0.2
whole milk	1 cup	9.0
whole wheat bread	1 slice	0.9

Hidden Sugar in Foods

Food Item	Portion Size	Approximate Sugar Content (Teaspoons)
Beverages		
Cola	12 oz	9
Ginger ale	12 oz	7½
Orangeade	8 oz	6
Tang	6 oz	5
Cranberry juice cocktail	6 oz	7½
Jams and Jellies		
Jelly	1 T	3
Jam	1 T	3½
Marmalade	1 T	3½
Apple butter	1 T	2
Candies		
Marshmallow	1	1½
Milk chocolate bar	1 1/5 oz	5
Chocolate fudge	1 cubic inch	4
Jelly beans	10	6½
Chewing gum*	1 stick	½
Cakes and Cookies		
Angel food cake*	1/12 of a 2-layer cake	6
Cheesecake	4 oz	6½
Chocolate cake (plain)	1/12 of a 2-layer cake	10½
Chocolate cake (iced)*	1/12 of a 2-layer cake	15
Jelly roll	2 oz	6½
Strawberry shortcake	1 serving	6
Browning (unfrosted)*	2"x2"x¾"	3
Chocolate cookies (frosted)	1	3
Ginger snaps	1	1½
Oatmeal cookies	1	1½
Sugar cookies	1	1
Cream puffs (iced)*	1 (custard filled)	5
Doughnut (plain)	1	2½
Doughnut (glazed)	1	6

*Joseph, L. "Foods and Drinks that Will Cause You Fewest Cavities." *Today's Health,* October 1973, pp. 41–43. Reprinted with permission from *Today's Health* magazine.

Dairy Products

Ice cream*	½ c	5–6
Chocolate milk	8 oz	4
Yogurt, fruit-flavored	1 c	6

Presweetened Cereals

Fruity Pebbles	1 oz (⅞ cup)	3
Sugar Smacks	1 oz (¾ cup)	4
Frosted Flakes	1 oz (⅔ cup)	3½

Desserts

Custard	½ c	2
French pastry	4-oz piece	5
Jello (without fruit)	½ c	4
Apple pie*	1 slice	12
Cherry pie*	1 slice (1/6 medium pie)	14
Cream pie	1 slice (1/6 medium pie)	4
Coconut pie	1 slice (1/6 medium pie)	10
Lemon pie	1 slice (1/6 medium pie)	7
Pumpkin pie*	1 slice (1/6 medium pie)	10
Raisin pie*	1 slice (1/6 medium pie)	13

Sugars and Syrups

Brown sugar	1 T	3
Granulated sugar	1 T	3
Molasses	1 T	3
Corn syrup	1 T	3
Chocolate syrup	1 T	3

Miscellaneous

Ice cream sundae	1 cup ice cream with 2 T chocolate syrup	16–18
Sherbet*	½ c	6–8
Peanut butter	2 T	½

*Joseph, L. "Foods and Drinks that Will Cause You Fewest Cavities." *Today's Health*, October 1973, pp. 41–43. Reprinted with permission from *Today's Health* magazine.

Plaque Fighters' Food Record

Instructions

1. Write down everything you eat and drink in the order in which you eat or drink it. Make sure to include *all* your snacks.
2. As you write down each food or drink, it is important that you record what the time is when you eat or drink. Also make sure to write down:
   a. The kind of food it is (such as "chocolate" milk or "peanut butter" sandwich or "tomato" juice).
   b. The amount of it you ate (a cup? a tablespoon? a slice? 12 ounces?).
   c. Anything you added to it (such as 1 pat of butter, 1 tablespoon of sugar, or ½ cup of milk).
   d. If it was prepared a certain way (such as fried, baked, broiled, or boiled).

Example:

WRONG   RIGHT

Breakfast		*Breakfast*	
	juice		½ cup tomato juice
	toast		1 slice toast with 1 teaspoon butter
Morning		7:30 a.m.	
	cereal		1 cup cornflakes with ½ cup milk and 1 teaspoon sugar
	orange		½ medium-sized orange

Morning		Morning	
Snacks		*Snacks*	1 stick spearmint gum
		10:00 a.m.	12-ounce Coke
		11:00 a.m.	1 small package peanuts
		11:30 a.m.	

Name _____ Day One

_____(Date _____)

Breakfast:

Morning snack:

Lunch:

Afternoon snack:

Dinner:

Evening snack:

Day Two

(Date _____)

Breakfast:

Morning snack:

Lunch:

Afternoon snack:

Dinner:

Evening snack:

Nutrition Knowledge Test
for Grade Five

Directions: Please choose the best answer for each question. Place your answer (the letter) in the space provided.

_____ 1. Which nutrient hardens bones and is not found in soft drinks?
   a. phosphorus
   b. vitamin C
   c. calcium
   d. iron

_____ 2. Susan grew five inches this year. Brian grew two inches this year. Which of these sentences is true?
   a. Susan grew too fast.
   b. Brian and Susan both grew too fast.
   c. Susan and Brian both grew too slow.
   d. Everyone grows at a different speed.

_____ 3. Which of the following does *not* affect how tall you will grow?
   a. the height of your parents and grandparents
   b. the amount of calcium in your diet
   c. the amount of other nutrients besides calcium in your diet
   d. the number of other children in your family

_____ 4. Suppose you had to quit eating all meat. What would happen to you?
   a. You could get your energy from sun tanning.
   b. You could get your energy from the plants you eat.
   c. You could make your energy from carbon dioxide and water.
   d. You would die.

_____ 5. Energy in our food comes from which nutrients?
   a. carbohydrates
   b. fats
   c. proteins
   d. all of the above

_____ 6. What jobs do enzymes perform in your body?
   a. They help get energy out of your food.
   b. They help you lose weight.
   c. They make energy out of water and carbon dioxide.
   d. They make minerals.

_____ 7. What is the best definition of basal metabolism?
    a. the digestion of food
    b. external body processes that make us move
    c. internal body processes that keep us alive
    d. exercise needed for health

_____ 8. Basal metabolism, digesting and absorbing foods, and physical activity are three ways that your body:
    a. uses energy.
    b. stays in good shape.
    c. makes vitamins and minerals.
    d. makes new cells.

_____ 9. Which three nutrients contribute Calories to your diet?
    a. proteins, fats, and vitamins
    b. proteins, carbohydrates, and fats
    c. fats, carbohydrates, and minerals
    d. vitamins, minerals, and proteins

_____ 10. Which of the situations below would result in a loss of body fat?
    a. Calorie input of 3,500 and Calorie output of 3,000
    b. Calorie input of 3,500 and Calorie output of 4,200
    c. Calorie input of 2,500 and Calorie output of 2,500
    d. Calorie input of 2,500 and Calorie output of 2,000

_____ 11. Which food contains the most fat?
    a. an orange
    b. a slice of whole wheat bread
    c. a cheeseburger
    d. a bowl of rice

_____ 12. Which meal is lowest in fat?
    a. a peanut butter sandwich, a glass of chocolate milk, and a banana
    b. a bowl of vegetable soup, 2 crackers, an apple, and a glass of skimmed milk
    c. a cheese sandwich, a glass of whole milk, and an orange
    d. a hamburger, a glass of skimmed milk, and potato chips

_____ 13. In which food would you expect to find complex carbohydrates?
    a. eggs
    b. meat
    c. potatoes
    d. yogurt

_____ 14. If you were trying to cut back on sugar, which would be your best choice of cereal?
    a. Trix
    b. Froot Loops
    c. Rice Chex
    d. Frosted Rice

_____ 15. Which of the following foods has the least amount of sugar?
   a. a cup of chocolate milk
   b. ½ cup of ice cream
   c. a piece of apple cake
   d. a whole carrot

_____ 16. Which food below would be the most orally hazardous?
   a. root beer
   b. chocolate milk
   c. ice cream
   d. caramels

_____ 17. Microorganisms are small living cells that all require _____ for growth.
   a. air
   b. darkness
   c. nutrients
   d. temperatures below 40° F.

_____ 18. How is the acid, which decays teeth, formed?
   a. bacteria + protein = acid
   b. bacteria + sugar = acid
   c. sugar + protein = acid

_____ 19. Susan needed 40 grams of protein each day for building and repairing body protein. What would happen to the extra 20 grams?
   a. It would be used for energy or stored as fat.
   b. It would be excreted.
   c. It would become a part of Susan's bones and teeth.
   d. It would be turned into vitamins.

_____ 20. What is one example of similar foods that are used in different cultures?
   a. tortillas in Mexico and crepes in France
   b. egg rolls in China and sauerkraut soup in Germany
   c. corn pudding in the United States and rye bread in Russia
   d. potato dumplings in Poland and Swiss cheese fondue in Switzerland

Answer Key to Nutrient Knowledge Test for Grade Five

1. c
2. d
3. d
4. b
5. d
6. a
7. c
8. a
9. b
10. b
11. c
12. b
13. c
14. c
15. d
16. d
17. c
18. b
19. a
20. a

The fourth in a curriculum series on nutrition for children, this volume for the fifth-grade level emphasizes the significance of diet and heredity in the growth process; the differences in energy requirements according to body size, metabolism, sex, age, environment, and physical activity; protein's role in tissue growth and the body's natural healing process; and the various cultural and environmental factors influencing diet.

Each of the twenty-one self-contained units encompasses a set of objectives, activities, evaluation material, and nutrition information for the teacher.

Optimum student interest is achieved through involvement with a number of original games, poems, stories, and cartoons in units entitled:

- Who's on First?
- Knee Bone Connected to the . . .
- How Tall is Your Family Tree?
- Snack Plaque Fighters
- It's a Small World

Lily Hsu O'Connell and James A. Rye, instructors of nutrition at Pennsylvania State University, work extensively in training dietitians. Dr. Paul E. Bell holds a doctorate in education and is associate professor of education at Pennsylvania State University.

Related Titles from Brigham Young University Press

**Nutrition in a Changing World—
A Preschool Curriculum**
Ellen S. Marbach, Martha Plass,
Lily Hsu O'Connell

Written for teachers with little or no training in nutrition, this guide helps children aged three through five experience a wide variety of foods through their senses of sight, sound, taste, smell, and touch.

**Nutrition in a Changing World—
A Primary Curriculum**
Ellen S. Marbach, Martha Plass,
Lily Hsu O'Connell

This valuable curriculum utilizes a variety of original poems, stories, and songs to teach children in grades one through three the basic four food groups, various nutrients, and their value to the body.

**Nutrition in a Changing World—
Grade Four**
Paul E. Bell, Lily Hsu O'Connell, James A. Rye

The focus of this volume for the fourth-grade level is to identify nutrients, their food sources, and why the nutrients are needed by the body. These activities foster the desire to maintain a healthy body by nutritionally balancing food choices.

Brigham Young University Press
Business Office, 205 UPB
Provo, UT 84602

Q: *Where do microorganisms grow?*

A: Microorganisms grow wherever the environment suits them. Have you ever seen bread mold? Mold needs the nutrients from bread, moisture, darkness, and a warm environment to grow. Microorganisms are found:

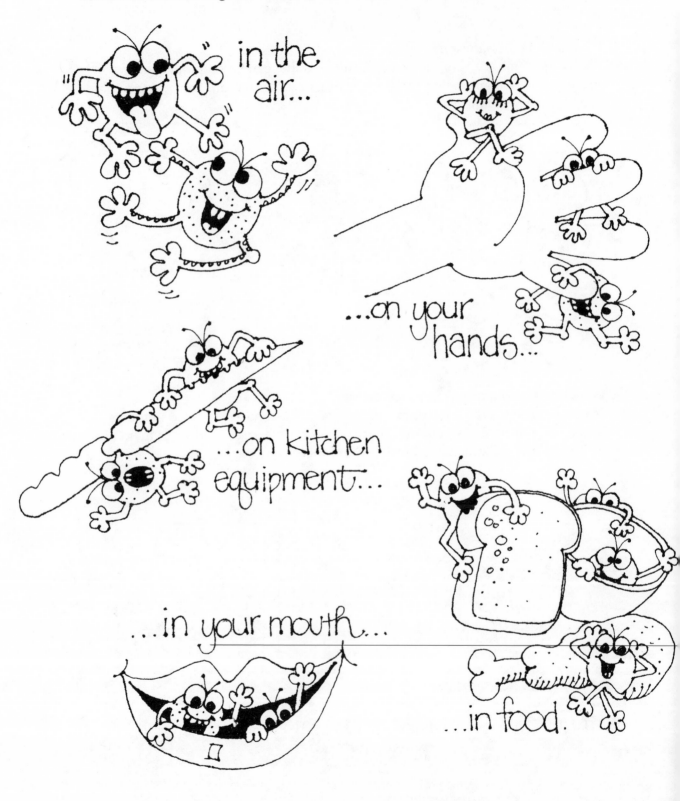

in the air...

...on your hands...

...on kitchen equipment...

...in your mouth...

...in food.